A Handbook for Personal Tutors

SRHE and Open University Press Imprint
General Editor: Heather Eggins

Current titles include:

A Handbook for Personal Tutors

Sue Wheeler and Jan Birtle

The Society for Research into Higher Education
& Open University Press

Published by SRHE and
Open University Press
Celtic Court
22 Ballmoor
Buckingham
MK18 1XW

and
1900 Frost Road, Suite 101
Bristol, PA 19007, USA

First Published 1993
Reprinted 1995

A catalogue record of this book is available from the British Library

ISBN 0 335 09954 8 (pb)
     0 335 09955 6 (hb)

Library of Congress Cataloging-in-Publication Data
Wheeler, Sue, 1948–
    A handbook for personal tutors / Sue Wheeler and Jan Birtle.
    p.   cm.
    Includes bibliographical references and index.
    ISBN 0-335-09955-6. — ISBN 0-335-09954-8 (pbk.)
    1. Tutors and tutoring—Great Britain—Handbooks, manuals, etc.
  2. Academic advisors—Great Britain—Handbooks, manuals, etc.
  3. College teaching—Great Britain—Handbooks, manuals, etc.
  4. Counselling in higher education—Great Britain—Handbooks,
  manuals, etc. I. Birtle, Jan, 1956– . II. Title.
  LC41.W47   1993
  371.3′94′0941—dc20   93–18530
                                                                  CIP

Typeset by Graphicraft Typesetters Ltd., Hong Kong
Printed in Great Britain by St Edmundsbury Press, Bury St Edmunds, Suffolk

Contents

Acknowledgements

We would like to thank several people for their help in producing this book, particularly Henry Miller who contributed his thoughts and ideas throughout, provided information about administrative structure of universities, and assisted in refining and proof reading the final draft. For their successful rescue when the computer went down, every author's nightmare, thanks to Nick Jurascheck and Fif. We thank Sue Rosten, Heather Espley and Gabrielle Kuhn von Burgsdorf for help with typing and Denise Griffin for her assistance with the index. We are indebted to past students and personal tutors of Aston and Birmingham universities who provided the original case material described in the book. We appreciated John Skelton cracking the whip occasionally in a friendly and encouraging way. We also acknowledge the help and support we gave each other throughout; despite occasional frustrations about our different styles we managed to put our contrasting skills to good use and we remain firm friends. Last, but not least, we thank Caroline Wheeler for the culinary treats that kept us going while we slaved over a hot word processor.

1

Setting the Scene

The need for a volume dedicated to an exploration of personal tutoring in higher education was identified through the work of the authors. We have a dual background in both student counselling and teaching in universities and are actively involved in personal tutoring. Viewing personal tutoring from these perspectives we became aware of the range of skills required to fulfil the role of the tutor and the inadequacy of preparation of most individuals engaged in this work. This volume aims to redress the balance by providing an introduction to personal tutoring based on student problems commonly encountered and a discussion of their treatment.

Aims of the authors

This is a source book for the use of personal tutors in higher education settings. This includes old and new universities, and colleges of higher education. We use the term university to describe all institutions of higher education. Some of the information will be useful for tutors working in other environments, including colleges of further education. Our major focus is on providing practical guidance for tutors, who come to this role with a variety of previous experiences and from a range of backgrounds. A few will already be familiar with emotional and psychological issues, but most will be more comfortable with pure academic work.

In Chapter 2 we outline the role of personal tutors and examine how they fit into the university setting. This includes an exploration of their duties and a description of other bodies involved in student welfare in a typical university. It is intended that this will provide tutors with a framework in which to function and assist them in finding out how their own universities cater for student welfare. With this information tutors are in a stronger position to refer students to appropriate supportive resources and thereby maximize student potential.

In order to facilitate the development of personal tutoring skills we have included a chapter on counselling skills. This outlines the basic principles of counselling practice and, although reading is no substitute for a training in counselling, Chapter 3 will aid tutors in the development of the skills of listening and responding to their students.

An aspect of the work of personal tutors is representing students' welfare interests through formal channels within the university. A section in Chapter 9 is devoted to describing how student welfare fits in to the administrative structure of a model university. We describe how the tutor can become involved in a more proactive way by interacting with this system in an effective manner.

We also provide a skeleton resource file for reference purposes in the Appendix. This includes suggestions for confidential advice and information services available in the community which students and tutors might wish to consult. An example is Aidsline, an organization which gives up-to-date information about sources of help for people who fear they may have been infected with Aids.

Confidentiality

The content of this volume is orientated around problems experienced by students during their higher education. In the examples provided we have drawn widely on our own practices and that of colleagues and ex-students in order to give a picture of authentic, real-life experiences. By choosing to do this we hope to ensure that relevant and useful information is presented.

We are sensitive of the need to preserve confidentiality for students and tutors and therefore have disguised details which might lead to identification of any individual. Names and courses are fictional and personal information has been omitted or altered. We have preserved the essence of the problems, as this is the core of the work, and have examined these with a view to helping personal tutors understand and respond to their students in a beneficial manner.

In this chapter we introduce a number of issues which are explored in detail in later sections of this volume. We start by outlining the context within which personal tutors work. This includes an introduction to the role of personal tutoring followed by an examination of contemporary changes within higher education which directly affect the work of tutors.

Who are personal tutors?

Personal tutors are members of the university staff with a role in the pastoral care of students. They are assigned a number of students, usually at least fifteen, to whom they have a particular responsibility.

Personal tutors are almost invariably members of the academic staff and are therefore also involved in teaching, research, and administration. The degree of investment of time and resources in personal tutoring is determined in part by the requirements of the university, who may state that each student should meet the tutor at a given time interval, say termly or annually. Requests from students for individual personal tutorials are often made in addition to this statutory minimum. For those who are failing academically the tutor may have extra meetings, either at the initiation of the tutor or the student. A further factor influencing investment in this work is based on the personal interest and involvement of individual tutors in the welfare of students, some giving more time to personal tutorial work than others.

Why do students need personal tutors?

The purpose of having a personal tutoring system is primarily to provide an anchor on which the support system of the university rests. The personal tutor is needed by all students, including those who enjoy a relatively straightforward passage through university. The existence of this system in itself may reduce student anxiety. Personal tutors also provide assistance for students in need, an important aspect of this work is attention to academic work when difficulties are experienced. There is also a welfare component and students may seek advice on a wide range of matters including housing, finance, emotional and relationship problems.

Students in higher education encounter a wide range of stresses or potential problems. Many are at a vulnerable stage in life. At the age of eighteen when the majority of students enter higher education they are experiencing physical and emotional changes related to late adolescent development. This is a time of internal turmoil for most people and students are no exception. As one student put it, 'I'd be all right if it wasn't for my hormones, they keep wrong-footing me.'

In addition to the stresses of adolescence students are often in the process of making a major transition, leaving their familiar homes and families and entering a strange environment where they know no one. Some quickly adapt, make new friends and settle in, whereas others feel isolated and lonely without the ready support of family and friends. There are additional pressures which arise from responsibilities including that of living on a limited budget, arranging accommodation, paying bills, and finding their way around a new place. These are practical difficulties often encountered for the first time when people enter higher education. Again individual responses to this vary, some students rise to the challenges posed whereas others have the experience of incapacitating stress.

Further difficulties are encountered when students begin academic work. The structure of study at universities is generally looser than in schools or colleges. Students are required to take more initiative for organizing time, obtaining course reading material, and handing in assignments or project dissertations. This can lead to problems, especially when students have previously been heavily reliant on teachers for academic direction. Faced with the task of organizing their own study schedules many students experience panic and as a result get behind with their work, thus generating further anxiety. Because help with time management and study skills can be of great benefit we devote Chapter 5 to an exploration of study problems and the development of these skills.

The academic life-cycle itself brings stresses at certain points during study. For instance starting a course at university, meeting deadlines for assignments, passing or failing examinations, and leaving are all associated with academic and emotional pressure. These are particular times when students are likely to need help.

In addition to hurdles brought about by course requirements some groups of students face specific stresses. Mature students returning to education after a period of time out may feel apprehensive about meeting the demands which will be made of them and the prospect of balancing these against domestic responsibilities. They are often relatively unfamiliar with academic study, or have distant memories of it, or are unsure how to operate the computerized library system.

Students from overseas face a major transition adapting to life in a new culture and in some instances may encounter hostility and alienation from their fellow students or neighbours. Postgraduate students are often working on research projects with limited supervisory support and as a consequence may experience isolation and despondency. Part-time students face the task of juggling demands on their time. Often they are concurrently studying, holding down a job, raising a family, or all of these. They may require assistance in prioritizing their time while keeping the standard of their academic work within acceptable limits.

Personal tutors are in direct contact with students and with the university system. This link can be used as a bridge between the students and the university services. Tutors inform students about where appropriate help can be gained and may refer students directly to services at times. On occasions when students are not coping despite considerable extra resources being provided tutors may be involved in helping them to make decisions about transferring to an alternative course, or even as a last resort leaving the university. This is often a difficult task in which the welfare of the student needs to be carefully balanced against the demands of the course.

In later chapters we will elaborate on the issues introduced here and provide illustrative examples of problems experienced within higher education settings. We will focus on the academic life-cycle and specific groups of students, exploring the nature of their difficulties and suggesting ways in which personal tutors can be of assistance.

What is the role of the personal tutor?

The central task of personal tutors is to assist students in fulfilling the requirements of their course. This may take the form of academic guidance when study problems are foremost. It also includes a responsibility for personal welfare, particularly when personal problems impinge on the capacity to study. In each of the groups of students introduced above special input is sometimes required. Study skills, library skills, networking, assertiveness training or student counselling may be indicated. It is the role of the personal tutor to find out what resources are accessible to students within the university in order to gain the most appropriate form of help for their students.

The personal tutor is part of a broad network of student support services within a university. The scope of this role varies between universities and is dependent on a number of factors including the nature and breadth of the student support services within the institution. This in itself is often a reflection of the degree of commitment which a specific university has made to student welfare.

In universities where student welfare is a high priority there will be an adequately staffed student counselling service, accommodation and welfare officers, medical and nursing personnel, chaplains and their equivalent representatives from a variety of religious denominations, and a careers advice centre. There will also usually be a senior member of the academic or administrative staff responsible for co-ordination of these services. Here the role of the tutor is primarily to provide a listening ear, to make limited interventions with students, and to act as a link with other student welfare services. The tutor in this model is in the front line with students and filters and directs them into the welfare system.

In stark contrast in universities where student welfare provision is a low priority personal tutors may find they are working in isolation with sole responsibility for the welfare of their students. In this setting the roles and expectations of tutors are more demanding, they will often find themselves acting in a number of capacities including academic adviser, friend, confidant, parent, advocate and counsellor.

We will outline the multiple roles of the personal tutor in detail in Chapter 2. To serve as an introduction we begin with some specific examples of problems presented to tutors.

Example: Duncan, a first year student, went to see his tutor in the second week of his course. He felt very anxious about starting at university and keeping up with the course work. During freshers week there had been a guided tour of the library which he attended, however because his mind was occupied by many worries at the time he was unable to take in what was being said. Consequently he felt lost in the library and did not know how to find references on his reading list. He was already getting behind with work and was afraid he would never catch up.

The tutor was able to reassure Duncan that the first couple of assignments did not carry much weight in terms of the overall course assessment. They were in part designed to help students begin academic work and learn to use the library. He went through the reading list with Duncan and explained how it was divided into books and journal articles. There were two forms of search system in the library and it was essential to know which one to access. He then suggested Duncan approach one of the library staff and indicated that their role encompassed showing people around and helping them learn how to use this facility. Duncan was immensely relieved and followed this course of action.

Here the tutor's role was to explain to the student how to interpret references, then to encourage him to seek help directly from the library staff. It was essential to inform Duncan that they would be happy to oblige, once armed with this information he felt sufficiently brave to ask for help. The tutor facilitated Duncan's interaction with the institution to mutual benefit, as Duncan was then able to use his time in higher education to good effect. As well as being rewarding for Duncan personally this improved the academic performance of a student, which is a measure of success for a university.

Example: Joanne came to see her tutor in a state of great distress. She had left the library late the previous evening and saw someone in the shadows who appeared to be watching her. It had been dark and she was unable to see clearly, but got the impression that a man began to follow her home. Frightened, she called in at the student's union where she met a friend who took her back to the hall of residence. The incident shocked her, she wondered if she could work late again in safety.

The tutor knew that previous assaults on students had occurred on campus and advised Joanne not to walk around on her own after dark. He also knew that there was a late bus service to the halls of residence which was co-ordinated through the students' union and which picked up from the library. He informed Joanne of this and told her about a self-defence course set up in order to minimize danger to students. He then discussed the problem with colleagues who agreed that his concerns should be taken seriously, they too had received a number of complaints from students about safety on campus. As a result a campaign to install better street lighting and frequent security patrols was launched and responded to by the university.

The tutor in this example again functioned in an advisory capacity, informing Joanne that she was probably putting herself at risk and helping her to maximize her personal safety. Simultaneously he took up the issue of the responsibility of the university in this respect. His campaign was supported, because there was widespread concern about security, and resulted in positive action being taken by the institution. He made an intervention at both a personal and an institutional level, and in doing so acted as a spokesperson for many concerned students and staff. In one sense he used Joanne's concerns to provide a feedback link to the university authorities. Because of his knowledge of the administrative machinery he was able to make this representation through effective channels. The process by which this was achieved is described in Chapter 9.

In the foregoing examples tutors were acting within their role. A difficulty which commonly affects tutors is knowing the appropriate boundaries of their work. Most tutors are keen to help their students. Sometimes it is difficult to know how far to go in these efforts and tutors may have a tendency to become over-involved. In the long term this is helpful to neither the tutors, who have considerable pressures on their time, nor to the students, who require more specialist help. The following example illustrates some of the pitfalls encountered when tutors extend their role outside their remit.

Example: A tutor contacted the student counselling service asking for urgent advice. She had seen one of her tutees earlier that day and was agitated and anxious about her. The student, Anna, had turned up in a very distressed state. In the past she had consulted the tutor on a number of occasions because of problems with her family. Her mother and father often argued. Her father drank heavily and, after a long period of domestic conflict, had moved out. During the previous weekend he returned and as a direct consequence her mother then left home. That day Anna had been to see her tutor and said that her father had returned home last night after an evening spent drinking. He then physically assaulted and raped Anna.

The tutor was horrified and told Anna she must report her father to the police and not under any circumstances return home that night. Instead she offered to put her up at her house, in the spare room. She also suggested that Anna should see a counsellor or her doctor.

The tutor was doing her best to help Anna. However Anna refused to take any action, she did not wish to involve the police, neither did she want to talk to anyone other than the tutor. She stayed for an hour, during which time the tutor tried to persuade her to seek alternative help, then left saying she was going back home to her father. The tutor was extremely worried about her and wondered if the counselling service could help, either directly or by advising the tutor what to do next.

The counsellor who took the call considered the situation carefully. Anna was over eighteen, she was therefore an adult and in the eyes of the law responsible for her own actions. This meant that the tutor would be breaching confidentiality if she informed the police, which was her first inclination. It appeared that Anna was in need of help and also aware of this in that she had sought out her tutor. The tutor had offered a sympathetic ear initially but was now saying that she was out of her depth, she felt Anna should see an experienced counsellor.

In response the counsellor reinforced the tutor's judgement that

Anna needed to see a specialist counsellor. He also explained that if Anna did not wish to do this there was little else that could be done to help her. The counsellor was able to supply information about the confidential nature of the student counselling service, which the tutor could pass on to Anna with a view to lessening her anxiety. He was also able to suggest alternative sources of support, including the Rape Crisis Centre who offered a confidential telephone advice service as well as a drop-in counselling facility.

The tutor was relieved that the counsellor thought she was acting well beyond her role. She had a further meeting with Anna where she emphasized that the help she could offer was limited. She could listen and try to understand Anna's difficulties and recognized that these were overwhelming. She thought Anna needed professional help and had looked into the options. It was now up to Anna to decide whether to follow any of these up and, if so, which.

Anna initially appeared to be rather stunned, her tutor had always been so understanding. She then realized that the tutor was speaking in earnest and taking her problem seriously. She recognized that she had reached the limits of whatever help the tutor could offer and must now go elsewhere. This frightened her, she trusted the tutor and had a lot of faith in her capacity to help. She had struggled to confide in her and was reluctant to start afresh with a stranger. However after some thought, and with trepidation, she eventually decided to consult a counsellor at the university.

Anna's tutor was grateful that she was relieved of the responsibility of being the sole person Anna relied on. While feeling she was being cruel in not helping her more the tutor also realized that this would be counter-productive in the long term as Anna needed more assistance than she could provide. Once Anna was seeing a counsellor the tutor was able to resume an appropriate and supportive relationship with her.

This example illustrates how well-meaning tutors can be drawn into situations in which they are acting outside the boundaries of their role. In this instance Anna's problems were of a serious nature, she was clearly emotionally disturbed and distressed and did not know which way to turn. It is the role of the tutor to be the first port of call on such occasions, to provide a listening ear as happened here. It is also the duty of tutors to ensure that students are given information about resources available in order that they are in a position to make an informed choice about seeking further assistance. Here the tutor was able to form a supportive relationship with Anna and listened and empathized well. Problems arose when Anna's difficulties became more severe and in parallel with this she became convinced that the tutor was the sole person able to offer help and support.

It is not the role of the tutor to offer overnight accommodation nor to provide direct advice for students, as did Anna's tutor. Students must find their own solutions to their problems. Anna herself must decide whether she wishes to take police action against her father; she is the person who is complaining she has been raped and who would be asked to give evidence in court against her father. It is possible she would be ostracized from her family if she decided to take legal recourse against him. As Anna would have to live with the consequences of her decision she is in the best position to make a judgement about what course of action to take.

Anna's tutor had worked within her role initially, however as Anna's difficulties became more intense the tutor became personally involved and lost her capacity to think objectively about her situation. Fortunately the tutor recognized this and sought advice from the student counselling service. Through this interaction she was able to re-establish the boundaries of her contact with Anna and to state the limitations of this work clearly without rejecting her student. With the encouragement of the tutor Anna was able to pluck up the courage to seek expert counselling.

We have used this early example because, although extreme in the difficulties presented, it provides a stimulus to examine the role, including the limitations, of personal tutors. This will be fully explored in later chapters. In the following section we will explore the setting in which personal tutors work.

The role of a university

Universities have two main functions, to educate people and to further research.

Higher, or tertiary, education takes place mainly within universities, which are responsible for teaching students and setting standards for assessment. A principle aspect of this task is the promotion of academic learning. It also encompasses the acquisition of technical and communication skills and, often a relatively neglected area, the personal development of students.

Educational techniques and theories are constantly evolving and universities are in the forefront of developments in this field. Likewise increasing attention is being paid to the evaluation of student learning and methods of teaching within higher education.

Increasingly universities are focusing on training initiatives in addition to pure academic study. Traditionally professional training for medicine and dentistry has taken place on undergraduate courses. The current trend is towards more specific training programmes being developed in collaboration with industry.

Universities are at the leading edge of new discoveries through their diverse research programmes. They are also centres of excellence in the development of research techniques and foster high standards of practice in pure academic research. Through postgraduate studentships specialist training in research methodology is undertaken.

The university within the community

Universities have long-standing links in the communities within which they are located. They take students for full-time degree courses which are usually of three or four years duration. Increasingly, these are connected with local industries and through these links sandwich courses, where students take time out of study for industrial placements, are organized. Conversely industries often send their employees to universities on short full-time or longer term part-time courses for further training. Access courses provide another channel between the local community and universities. They are designed to provide a route into higher education for individuals with limited previous educational attainments. Moving further afield universities regularly take students from many overseas countries, thereby extending their training role from a local to an international arena.

On the research front there are increasing numbers of joint ventures which are organized by university departments in conjunction with industry. In return for funding universities offer their expertise plus staff time and the use of equipment on an agreed basis. The questions being explored in this collaborative manner are usually more practically based than pure academic research and results are directly utilized in the industry which sponsored them.

Current trends in higher education

There are many changes occurring within higher education at present which have an impact across the entire spectrum of university activities, including personal tutoring. In order to provide a context for the changes in this area we will outline some of the more far reaching changes.

Funding

Universities are mainly funded by central government through the University Funding Council. Other sources of finance include research councils, student fees, endowments, and consultancy fees. From a central pool of money individual universities are allocated portions. Within each university further divisions are made as the overall budget is apportioned to faculties, departments, and research centres. These to some extent reflect the direction of central government and are partly determined by priorities within the given institution and success in bidding for research funds. Policies and priorities on which funding arrangements are made change in line with the overall government strategy of the day. This is influenced by party politics, by the current national balance, and by the principle needs and demands of the influential sectors of the community at large.

As well as directing the funding of universities the Government has an influence on student finances via their policies on student grants, through which they determine eligibility criteria and the degree of financial support which is awarded. In periods of recession and high unemployment this tends to be cut back, leaving students on tight budgets and for the most part unable to supplement their income by vacation employment. Loan schemes have been introduced to bypass some of these difficulties but again when unemployment is high students may have difficulty ultimately repaying such loans.

Increasing student enrolment

At the time of writing many changes are occurring in higher education following major shifts in government funding policies. These consist of a reduction in the proportion of central government support and increased competition for research funding. Apart from research funding the trend is towards financial allocation being principally determined by the numbers of students enrolled within a given university, apportioned to departments on the basis of their recruitment. This has had the effect of some departments increasing student intakes to courses in order to maintain a reasonable level of financial allocation. This expansion is taking place without an equivalent increase in academic staffing levels, placing pressure on the teachers.

The expanding student population has an impact on students as well as on staff. There is increased pressure to find suitable accommodation, this is already at a premium near most university sites. On campus teaching space is often cramped and heavily used and classes are large, reducing the personal contact between lecturers and students. Both catering and library facilities tend to be congested, resulting in students having difficulty obtaining basic essentials such as food, course texts, and even in some cases beer. These pressures are likely to be felt by personal tutors, as students relay their worries and concerns within their personal tutorials.

Changes in teaching practice

One possible response to increasing student enrolment is to enlarge class size and to make the lecture the principle forum for teaching. This would ensure that course material could be adequately covered. However it is increasingly recognized that the acquisition of knowledge in itself is of limited value. What is required in the present day is a combination of skills and knowledge, resulting in the emergence of graduates with practical as well as knowledge based competencies.

An example is provided in medical education where courses are traditionally heavily biased towards the reading and retention of information. This approach has limitations in a world where the current state of knowledge is rapidly changing because of advances in treatment approaches derived from medical research. Information rapidly becomes redundant and is therefore of little value to the practising doctor. More crucial is the capacity to obtain accurate up-to-date details about diagnostic techniques and treatment options, including their likely success rates and side effects.

In tandem with this change of emphasis patients are becoming more vocal and questioning decisions about treatment. Thus the doctor of today can no longer rely on authority and status as a defence against ignorance. Patients wish to be better informed and expect to be able to discuss decisions with their doctors. Communication skills are essential to today's doctor and increasingly are being incorporated into training. These skills include oral, written, and information technology competencies. As medical education moves towards focusing on communication skills, a compensatory reduction in other aspects of the course content is required. To date this is not occurring. Without this balance being redressed students are in danger of being swamped with ever-expanding curriculum requirements resulting in over-load and exhaustion.

The model of changes in medical education is echoed in other subjects. Overall there is a need for realignment of the educational process and evaluation of methods of teaching in higher education. Whereas the traditional lecture may be a relatively efficient forum for didactic teaching, where knowledge is relayed to an audience, skills cannot usually be taught in this manner. For learning of this nature to be valuable active participation is essential. Despite the pressures of increased student numbers the small group remains the most effective forum for the development of skills, where students practice under the supervision of a teacher.

Participative learning in this setting requires that students become more actively involved in and responsible for their own education. The teacher is a guide rather than a source of information and helps students direct their questioning processes. Ultimately the aim of this form of educational initiative is that students will emerge as graduates capable of continuing independent learning, as they will have learned how to go about the task of learning.

The altered focus in teaching and learning emphasis also has an impact on students, who may be anxious and suspicious about the shift in expectations of their teachers. Some express anger and frustration in the face of being required to be more actively involved in directing their own learning, particularly when this approach is encountered for the first time in higher education. Other initiatives which challenge students and teachers alike include the introduction of computer assisted learning, increasing use of multiple choice questions, and reduction in staff–student contact.

Academic audit

Changes in government policy and accountability have resulted in a need for universities to audit their work. In addition to being answerable for student enrolment they are increasingly required to ensure that their work in both teaching and research is of a high standard. Quality is a key word, and attempts are being made to define what is meant by quality in university enterprises. As part of this process the work of academic staff is regularly appraised, individuals negotiate goals with their line managers and are answerable for any shortfall in performance. One aspect of appraisal is that increased efficiency in the use of staff time is demanded.

Increased efficiency is required in teaching, where the changing focus of higher education requires audit, or regular evaluation, of the teaching process. Initiatives to examine teaching efficiency and the aims of higher education are constantly evolving. Curriculum revision has become an ongoing process and is accompanied by the definition and constant refinement of specific learning objectives. While time becomes both more scarce and accountable there is a constant striving towards the maintenance of standards, which in a period of limited resources is achieved largely by introducing efficiency measures. Thus the role of the academic teacher is altering, the expenditure of time is closely scrutinized and balanced against results. Academic audit is now a major driving force behind changes in educational strategies, and one that is here to stay.

These trends have an impact on academic staff, especially those who have not previously been asked to evaluate their teaching methods. For many these changes bring feelings of uncertainty, discomfort, and unease, plus the pressure of extra forms to complete. Adaptation is required and is not always easy. Meanwhile parallel developments are taking place within the research arena where the need for efficiency is leading to increasingly focused research aims and a tendency towards large-scale collaborative research programmes. Again these require changes in the working practice of academics.

Appraisal of academic work has resulted in pressure to produce research publications which acts to reduce the time available for teaching and contact with students.

Impact on personal tutors

A major effect of increased student numbers which is of central relevance to this book is on the personal tutoring system. Whereas a select group of academics previously acted as personal tutors it is generally the case that almost all now have responsibilities for student welfare, often without an increase in time allocation for this work. Academics will usually have approximately fifteen students under their wings and as student enrolment continues to rise this figure will increase. Tutors have varying degrees of responsibility for their students but typically will be expected to see each one individually on a termly basis, a not inconsiderable investment of time.

It is possible that in the future tutors will be asked to audit their personal tutorial contact with students. Already in some departments where there are specific requirements that students are seen regularly tutors are encouraged to keep notes of meetings. As the trend towards academic audit continues to evolve the role of the tutor is likely to be evaluated in line with other academic work.

Anticipating this development tutors are well advised to attempt some form of self-evaluation of their tutoring role. This might simply consist of an audit of the time spent on pastoral care each term. Once basic information is assembled there is potential to introduce efficiencies and tutors themselves are in the optimal position to take a proactive role in such developments.

> *Example:* An early task of tutors is to ensure that students meet them. Students will need to be orientated to the work of the tutor and how to go about making an appointment. Tutors could see each of their tutees individually, in the first term, in order to relay this information. An alternative model which results in a more efficient use of time would be to meet the students as a group. In this setting the tutor can say something about the tutoring role, ask the students to introduce themselves, inform them how to make an appointment, and present information about other student support services available. Time spent in ensuing individual tutorials can then be used to focus on the particular problems experienced by their tutees. Students can also be given an opportunity to ask questions and to meet their peers. A further advantage of discussing common concerns in this way is that they may feel more able to approach their peers for support and help.

The rewards of personal tutoring

Personal tutoring is not necessarily always an onerous task. For some academics it is a valuable form of contact with students. By meeting with students on an individual basis tutors are able to develop a relationship of trust and gain a perspective which would be difficult to otherwise see. In the privacy of personal tutorials tutors are afforded insights into the current life-styles and concerns of students. The tutor may receive valuable feedback about courses and the university system which can be used to enhance the quality of education.

One of the most rewarding aspects of being a tutor is getting to know individual students and facilitating both their academic and personal development. During the time spent at university considerable intellectual and personal growth takes place which can be both exciting and stimulating to observe. A little input from a tutor can go a long way in this respect and throughout the remainder of this volume we will present examples of interventions which have resulted in positive changes for students, alongside a few warnings about the pitfalls of this role.

2

The Role of the Personal Tutor

In most institutions of higher education in Britain students are assigned to a member of staff who takes some responsibility for their welfare. This role is given a variety of titles including moral tutor, welfare tutor, mentor, and course tutor. We prefer the term 'personal tutor' because it implies that there is a responsibility for students' personal well-being as well as other duties that may be incorporated into the role.

We define a personal tutor as a member of academic staff whose role and function may include responsibilities:

- to facilitate the personal development of their tutees;
- to monitor the progress of their tutees;
- to provide a link between the student and the university authorities;
- to be a responsible adult within the organization, in whom the student can confide;
- to intervene with the university authorities on behalf of their tutees.

The role of personal tutor in our institutions of higher education has a long tradition. Oxbridge colleges have always had a tutorial system with a specific member of staff assigned to each student to guide them on the path through their degree course. This member of staff is described as a moral tutor and traditionally gives guidance on personal and moral issues, as well as academic support. When the age of majority was twenty-one years moral tutors had a responsibility *in loco parentis*, providing 'parental' guidance to young people living away from home.

The model of education and the pastoral care system of Oxford and Cambridge universities has had a historically significant influence on higher education throughout Britain although this has declined during the past two decades with the expansion of higher education (Halsey, 1991; Tapper and Salter, 1992). The Oxbridge moral tutor tradition had its original roots in institutions dedicated to training the clergy and was perpetuated more widely in universities in the interests of fostering 'a gentlemanly elite'. By the mid-twentieth century a diluted Oxbridge tradition had colonized most universities epitomized by emphasis on the civilizing influence of halls of residence and contact with academic staff, some of whom would have been called personal tutors. This tradition continues to be diluted as the movement towards mass provision of higher education gathers pace with the abolition of the binary divide and an increased emphasis on research.

In the past universities and colleges had few welfare resources other than academic staff, a chaplain and perhaps a matron. Students who approached these individuals for help would receive guidance which was largely didactic or prescriptive in nature. There are always individuals who have a natural talent for understanding and helping others but for those who were not blessed with these gifts there was no training available to help them acquire such skills. The British traditionally manifest a 'stiff upper lip' attitude and institutions of higher education were no exception. Even when problems were perceived as having a psychological dimension there were limited specialist treatment centres available, thus the brunt of responsibility fell on personal tutors and matrons. The system relied heavily on authoritarian control manifest in rules and regulations, backed up by kindly advice. The stigma associated with psychological distress was much greater than in contemporary society and would effectively deter many individuals from seeking help.

Today the scenario in higher education has changed dramatically. There are many more students in the system from a diversity of cultures, educational and social backgrounds. Attitudes have changed with respect to asking for help and support. The notion 'succeed or drop out' has been challenged by the high cost of student wastage and, once selected into the system, students are now encouraged to complete their studies.

Simultaneously the pressures on staff have become greater. Changes in funding for higher education have imposed rigorous demands for research output together with increased teaching loads. As a result time available for consultation with students has been drastically reduced. This has to some extent been balanced by the introduction of specialist welfare and counselling centres in many institutions of higher education. However students will inevitably continue to seek help from academic staff who are familiar and in regular contact with them. The manner in which personal tutors and other specialist advisory services link up will be explored in Chapter 8. Here we will describe the numerous roles which personal tutors may fulfil with respect to their students.

Students experience a variety of problems during their courses and approach tutors with a range of expectations. They may be looking for a parent substitute, friendship or academic advice. Thus the personal tutor may represent a number of different, sometimes overlapping, figures to the student. It is important that the personal tutor keeps this in mind and responds sensitively, but not collusively, to the student. To aid personal tutors we present an overview of their multiple roles accompanied by a description of potential traps and pitfalls which is designed to help them negotiate these somewhat tricky waters.

Personal tutors consciously or unconsciously seek a comfortable role model to use in their relationship with students and individuals will make various choices based on their own experience, inclination and expectations. Some choose or are expected to adopt the following:

Friend
It is not unusual for the role of 'friend' to be adopted. The implication is that the tutor has an easy, informal, two-way relationship with tutees based on mutual liking and respect without the burden of power, responsibility and authority. However this is not altogether realistic as tutors do hold responsibility and it is unlikely that they would want to be friends with all of their tutees. What happens to those who they do not like or with whom they would not choose to spend their time? Friendship is a two-way process of give and take founded on equality. While students may appreciate the kind of friendship that makes them special and gives them extra attention, the question is whether they are able to contribute equally to the relationship. Other students may feel left out if they are not included in the friendship group.

For a 'friend' role to be successfully adopted it needs to be clearly defined as a special form of friendship in which boundaries and responsibilities are specified. This must be adopted with the whole group of tutees, rather than with a few special individuals. The tutees need to know what is acceptable behaviour in terms of visiting and telephoning the tutor and need to be assured of confidentiality when it is appropriate.

Adviser
There are many instances when tutors become advisers because they have specialist knowledge of some areas. For example tutors should know, or be able to find out, about the functioning of the institution, its rules, regulations and expectations. They have experience of how the department or school has dealt with student problems in the past, which provides a basis for advice. They also have specialist knowledge about their subject or vocation. They may, however, be consulted about personal difficulties which demand a different kind of attention and require them to be reflective and non-judgemental. It is quite reasonable for tutors to give advice in the areas of their competence but important that they remember that they are not experts on someone else's life!

Referral agent
One way in which a tutor may offer advice is to refer a student to another agency when appropriate. It is an essential aspect of a tutor's responsibilities to know what is available within the institution and to have some awareness of wider community facilities. An institutional resource directory should be available to all tutors. For example, if a student is undecided about future career plans it would be appropriate to refer them to the careers service. At the same time it is good practice to arrange to see the student following the interview to keep in touch and review progress. The personal tutor's role as a referral agent provides an essential link between the

student body and the network of support systems within the institution. This topic is discussed further in Chapter 8.

Academic assessor

When a personal tutor also has an assessment role the relationship with students will be affected. Assessors are seen as authority figures upholding the rules and standards of the institution. Students may be reluctant to discuss their anxieties about the course or their personal limitations when the tutor is involved in its assessment. Acknowledging weakness in a particular area is the first step towards improvement, however this can be difficult with the person who is ultimately the judge.

Disciplinarian

There may be instances when personal tutors are required to be very firm with their tutees or even to invoke disciplinary proceedings against them.

> *Example:* Robert was a difficult student with many social problems. He could not make friends with other students and was often isolated. He constantly sought the attention of members of staff to whom he would pour out his troubles. This was acceptable and understandable at first but continued to the point that he was regularly taking up many hours of staff time. A case discussion was held to decide how best to help him because there were several manifestations of his problems which affected other people. It was decided that his personal tutor would take on a central co-ordinating role to help the student recognize and control his behaviour. This involved the personal tutor being firm and clearly spelling out to Robert that his antisocial behaviour in lectures was unacceptable and that it had to stop, otherwise he would be reported to the head of department with disciplinary consequences. The personal tutor also undertook to see Robert once a week to give him support and listen to his concerns. All other members of staff were asked to refer the student back to his personal tutor and not to give him more than a couple of minutes of their time when demands were made.

In this instance the attempt to contain Robert's behaviour worked well although it made many demands on the personal tutor. The student developed a strong relationship with the tutor and seemed to recognize that his needs for attention were being met by someone who was kind but firm.

Academic

The personal tutor may also be an academic tutor with responsibility for a specific subject. This need not conflict with the pastoral function as long as students are clear about the dual role. To aid this separation it may be helpful to give personal tutorials a specific time slot rather than tacking them on to the end of academic tutorials. An academic tutor will have knowledge about a student's level of achievement in their subject which can be put to use in the tutorial. It is important not to judge the student by their performance in one subject as this may not be representative of their overall standard.

There may be times when a student formally contracts with their tutor to have regular meetings to help them with academic work. This may occur because student requests specific help with study skills or time management, or because an exam board formally asks a personal tutor to take on such a role.

Parent

Although in higher education students are usually over the age of eighteen, and therefore legally adult, some personal tutors identify with parents when circumstances arise that pose the moral question of what kind of help they would wish for their own teenage children. At the same time some students seek help as they would from their parents. Young people often provoke anxiety in others which can leave the personal tutor with a dilemma about whether to take action.

> *Example:* Albert was twenty years old and had a history of depression. He failed to report in a final examination. His personal tutor was very concerned about him and went to his flat to find out what had happened. Here the tutor decided to act on his anxiety and check that Albert was well. It is debatable whether visiting the flat was going beyond his role and responsibility. Perhaps he should have sent a note inviting Albert to see him. However in this instance the response was based on his knowledge of Albert and necessary for the tutor's peace of mind.

There is often a great conflict for personal tutors regarding contacting parents when students have a serious problem.

> *Example:* Penny was epileptic. Her condition was under control when she was careful with her diet and drinking but when she indulged in too much alcohol she had fits which her flatmates had to deal with. They were frightened by the severity of the fits and contacted the medical centre who consulted Penny's tutor. A decision was made that Penny's condition was too much responsibility for her flatmates and that it would be better for Penny to live at home with her parents who lived nearby. The tutor confronted Penny with the problem but she flatly refused to tell her parents about her recurrent fits.
>
> The tutor and the doctor had to consider whether it was in Penny's best interest to inform her parents without her consent. They decided that the problem should be tackled in another way as Penny was an adult who had to make her own decisions. The university residences office was consulted and Penny was told that she could no longer continue to live in Hall because no one there was able to take responsibility for her health and safety. This threw the problem back onto Penny who eventually decided to consult her parents for help.

It would have been tempting to contact her parents but unethical even in these difficult circumstances, although the alternative course of action was not pleasant either. Some students actively look for a substitute parent and the tutor needs skill to help students find their independence without seeming to reject them.

Advocate

Personal tutors may have instances in which they are required to be advocates for their tutees. For example, they may be asked to represent a student in court or at an exam board.

Example: A student failed her final examinations although she was academically very able. Her tutor had been in close contact with her all year as she struggled to cope with her feelings about her parents' separation. Her distress was considerable because of her involvement in a family incident that had triggered the separation. The tutor knew many details concerning the circumstances of the problem but did not disclose these when she was asked to speak on behalf of the student at the exam board. However she did pledge her support for the student, confirmed there were genuine personal difficulties, and asked the board to view the case with sympathy.

Example: Simon was accused of having an illegal homosexual relationship with another student when they were both under age. Simon was summoned to court and his personal tutor accompanied him to be a character witness.

The support of a member of the academic staff who knows the student concerned is invaluable. Particularly when students are in a strange city, without their home support system, the tutor's support role is vital.

Counsellor

There may be times when personal tutors can give practical advice or guidance to their tutees. There are also likely to be instances when it is appropriate to use active listening or counselling skills, to help students explore and clarify their problems for themselves.

Example: Just before his final examinations Chris approached his personal tutor with a problem. His father had been arrested and imprisoned for sexually assaulting Chris's seven year-old niece. Chris was shocked and horrified, unable to concentrate on his academic work and about to go home to give support and comfort to his mother. The personal tutor found this scenario very distressing, unaccustomed as he was to dealing with personal issues. Chris also found it difficult to approach his personal tutor but the circumstances were such that he had no choice. The personal tutor supported Chris to the best of his ability by listening and trying to convey understanding. He subsequently referred him to the counselling service.

Chris's tutor did not consider himself to be skilled in counselling, but in this instance his compassion enabled him to listen and help Chris to make decisions about his next steps. Chris needed someone in the university to give him permission to be upset and neglect his work for a while. He would have jeopardized his examination prospects had he gone off without giving any indication of his circumstances.

Personal tutors act as a bridge between the student and the academic system. They have a choice about how far they extend their role and about how much time they give to listening and understanding students' difficulties. Some choose to deal with only the practical aspects of academic work and in doing so may deny students the help and support they need to deal with underlying sources of their problems. Personal tutors should at least be able to listen in an empathic way to their students' concerns and refer them on to the college counsellor or other agency for specialist help.

Teacher
Personal tutors may be involved in the student's academic studies as lecturers or academic tutors. They may also take on the role of teaching in a more general way, for instance by facilitating the development of writing or study skills.

> *Example:* Judy was a mature student who had gained a place on an undergraduate programme through the Access scheme [which is described in Chapter 6]. She was bright and enthusiastic but very disappointed with the poor mark she received for her first essay. She confided this to her personal tutor who reviewed the essay with her, even though it was not in her subject area. Through the time and attention given, and by drawing on relevant literature, Judy's essay writing and other study skills were vastly improved.

The development of study skills is described more fully in Chapter 5.

Careers adviser
Some students have a clear idea of what they want from their university studies and subsequent career, whereas others may require counselling and guidance. Personal tutors who give space to their tutees to reflect on their plans for the future will be greatly appreciated. There may not be space within a course for consideration of career opportunities and some tutors may be able to give guidance and advice. When referral is made to the careers service it is good practice to invite the student back to report on their discussions and progress. Careers work lends itself well to a group setting as will be discussed later in this chapter.

Referee
At the end of a student's academic course they are likely to want to take up employment, for which they will require references. On some courses

students develop close relationships with their course tutors who would subsequently be able to write meaningful references, other courses may be more fragmented with little personal contact being made with academic staff. In these instances the personal tutor may be asked to provide references. For this and other reasons it is good practice to keep brief notes of tutorial sessions, to be used by the tutor as a reminder of the student at a later date, or in case of dispute or appeals about conduct or performance.

Confidant

Personal tutors can be put into the role of confidant by students, which can be uncomfortable. Ultimately all students must acquire independence and move on into employment or other activity with maturity and confidence. While it is important that personal tutors take an interest in their tutees, boundaries to this involvement are important. Personal counselling is a legitimate activity for a tutor but being the person that the tutee turns to in all circumstances extends the role too far.

> *Example:* Frieda was a very insecure young person who had difficulty surviving away from her parents, to whom she was very attached. She quickly latched on to her personal tutor as someone she could relate to, and set him up as a parental figure and confidant. At first the tutor saw himself in a supportive role and was sympathetic to her needs, making time for her whenever she approached him. However after a few weeks he became aware that her relationship with him was the sole friendly contact she had at college and that she was using him to express all her complaints, irritations and observations. He realized that their relationship had overstepped the role that he would expect to have as a personal tutor and sought advice from the college counsellor.

Although Frieda's tutor started out being helpful and supportive to her, he soon realized that she was demanding too much of him. He was wise to discuss the problem with a counsellor as this process helped him understand Frieda's behaviour and subsequently enabled him to draw more appropriate boundaries between them. Frieda, for her part, needed to become aware of her difficulties so that she could develop her independence and find confidants from among her peer group.

Institutional change agent

There are certain circumstances in which it is appropriate for personal tutors to act on behalf of their personal tutees and influence the university to change a practice that causes specific difficulties for students. Many institutions of higher education are bureaucratic and sometimes decisions are made which do not take full account of their impact on students. This is explored further in Chapter 9.

Boundaries

No two personal tutors are likely to perform their duties with relation to their tutees in the same way. Within this role there is room for considerable diversity of practice but there are also some boundaries that should be considered and adhered to. For example earlier in this chapter we have discussed the role of the personal tutor *in quasi loco parentis*. It is common practice for tutors to invite their tutees to an informal gathering at some time during the academic year either within the college, at a local pub, or sometimes in their own home. While there are circumstances when it can be valuable to invite students to tutors' homes, such invitations should be issued with caution. Students can be rivalrous with each other therefore it is important to avoid favouritism. If one student is invited as part of the personal tutor's work the whole group of tutees should be treated in the same way. Members of academic staff are authority figures, and students need to know where they stand with them. They are likely to feel secure when the tutor's behaviour is consistent.

The relationship

In order for personal tutoring to be effective there must be a relationship between tutor and student. For this to exist the two must meet, preferably in a comfortable and private setting which preserves the boundaries of confidentiality. Although this may appear to be stating the obvious it is not unusual for students to complete their course without ever meeting or speaking to their personal tutor!

Ideally we recommend that academic staff should have no more than fifteen tutees at any one time. Most academic staff members are personal tutors. In any institution there will be staff who have chosen this profession because they enjoy the stimulation of teaching and the challenge of inspiring young people with their subject. They feel comfortable with students and enjoy both the formal and informal contact with them. On the other hand, there will also be a core of staff who are there primarily because of interest in their subject and the opportunities for research, and by whom students are sometimes perceived as a nuisance. The quality of the relationship between staff and students is likely to be very different in each of these scenarios. However if the personal tutorial system of an organization is publicly valued and regarded as the backbone of the pastoral care system it is possible for attitudes to change. Even the most unlikely staff members can be encouraged to give what they can to make the system work.

Tutorial meetings

We recommend that formal appointments be made with tutees at least once each term and that these meetings be scheduled for half an hour.

Personal tutors should also make it clear to their tutees where and how they can be contacted at other times. It is advisable for tutors to set aside a specific time each week when they are available. It is also important to ensure that students know where to go in an emergency. This and other organizational issues are discussed further in Chapter 10.

The academic life-cycle

The role of the tutor varies in response to changes in the needs of students as they progress through their academic career. This section will look at the demands made on tutors at different times in the academic life-cycle, a subsequent section includes an exploration of how some of these demands can be catered for in a group setting.

At the beginning of a course students may need help to settle in. Later on they require opportunities to monitor their progress through the course and some will need help with the ending process. Personal tutors can have a substantial impact in easing the path towards adjustment through these different stages.

First year induction

The initial meeting between a student and their personal tutor is crucial as it sets a precedent for the conduct of their relationship. Personal tutors may meet their tutees for the first time in a group or as individuals. When this meeting is held early in the academic year the students will be going through a process of adjustment to their new surroundings and circumstances. This is an excellent time for the tutor to set ground rules for the personal tutoring relationship. First impressions are powerful therefore it is important to work at establishing good communication in this initial meeting. It is often useful to start by taking an active interest in the student. Some open-ended questions which may be helpful include:

• Tell me something about yourself.
• How do you feel about being here?
• How does the college differ from your school?
• What do you expect from your experience here?
• What kind of extra curricula activities do you expect to become involved with?
• Is there anything that you are anxious about with respect to being a student?
• What personal resources do you have that might help you to settle in here and enjoy yourself?
• Have you thought about what kind of career you would like to follow?

It is also important to discuss guidelines for the use of tutorials and the tutorial relationship. This will vary depending on the role definition determined by the institution. A crucial aspect is the provision of a pastoral link between the student and the university.

It is important to stress that students are expected to attend tutorials. Tutorial time is sometimes mistakenly discussed in terms of dealing with 'problems'. It is more constructive to present it in the context of support and development. The issues of confidentiality need clarification, the tutor emphasizing that the degree of confidentiality in personal tutorials is high, although when matters of life and death are involved it may be broken.

Beware of saying, 'if you have any problems, come and see me'. It sounds helpful but also implies that problems are the only passport to a meeting. 'Problems' will be interpreted differently by individuals. To a student who is dependent on others for support and guidance in all matters a trivial issue can be a problem. Another, who has been taught to be independent and proud, would need to be in a desperate situation before they would describe themselves as having a problem.

First year second term

'How is everything going?' would seem an appropriate opening question at this stage, followed by careful listening to the response. This includes paying attention to non-verbal communication and intonation which may give clues about unspoken issues. By the end of the first term the average student will have got used to the college environment, made some friends, and have some idea whether they are on the right course. By the beginning of the second term they should even have started to do some work! If they have not yet managed to do any of these, warning bells should be ringing. The personal tutorial can be used to check out the student's progress or lack of it. This is aided by the tutor asking a few tactful questions pertaining to various areas of a student's life. It is important when doing this to avoid bombarding the student with questions followed by advice. In Chapter 3 we enlarge on counselling skills.

First year third term

Exams! Many students take examinations in their stride and are unconcerned by them. Others become anxious and make heavy weather of the whole process. It is important to be aware of this even when it is not the focus of a tutorial. Projects, placements, accommodation and second year options may also be on the agenda at this time. Many students are faced with the additional worry of supporting themselves during the summer vacation now that all government financial support has been withdrawn.

Increasingly financial problems are likely to be a feature of students' lives. They may need to be reminded of the network of support systems available to help them within the university, as described in Chapter 8.

Second year

By the second year students have a fair idea about standards and expectations. They also have more awareness of their personal abilities and limitations with respect to study methods, aptitude and interest in their subject. Any of these areas could be the focus of a review session in tutorials.

The second term of the second year is often a difficult time for students. It is winter, post-Christmas excitement, and the reality of hard work leading up to the summer exams looms large. By this time students have made a substantial commitment to their course which is fine if it is right for them but rather daunting if it is not. It can be the time when an aspect of a student's life that is not going well comes to a head, and this may culminate in depression, anxiety, or the threat of opting out.

> *Example:* Rupert was a second year pharmacy student. He visited his tutor early in the second term of the second year to report that he was intending to leave the university. He said at first that he was not enjoying the subject and feared that he would not be able to pass the second year examinations. The tutor referred to Rupert's academic record which was just about adequate. Had he been less skilled as a tutor he might have tried to persuade Rupert that he would be able to pass his examinations but he chose to try to help Rupert identify for himself whether that was really the main source of his concerns. Rupert was a quiet and apparently shy young man who did not find it easy to confide in anyone. The tutor suggested to Rupert that his shyness with people could be part of the problem and this comment enabled his tutee to express his concerns about his social life and relationships. Rupert was referred to the counselling service. As part of the therapy he was helped to recognize and accept his homosexuality and was subsequently able to complete his course successfully.

At this stage in a student's academic life the realization dawns that if they are not already integrated with university life and their course it is unlikely to happen, unless there are substantial changes. If social expectations of university life have not been fulfilled, disillusion and disappointment may ensue. The disappointment may be about academic or personal issues, the latter frequently relating to adolescent sexuality. Chapter 4 expands on this theme.

Third year

The preoccupations of the third year include finals, career, preparing for separation from the institution, finding a partner and financial problems.

Personal tutors can provide a valuable sounding board for discussion or guidance about any of these issues. Final examinations can be the recognizable stimulus that creates enormous anxiety for students. However anxiety about examinations can be a symptom hidden behind which is anxiety about the responsibilities of adulthood or leaving the institution. Final examinations can be the key to the door of the rest of your life and, for some, the level of responsibility entailed is not welcome. Fear of success can be as much of a problem as fear of failure, although more difficult to identify and understand.

> *Example:* Sheila was a final year engineering student. She had always been an excellent student and was expected to achieve a first class degree. Two days before her final examinations she went to see her tutor to announce that she was leaving before taking her final examinations. He was shocked and horrified by her announcement, but managed to contain himself enough to listen to her and take her anxieties seriously. She was saying very clearly that she did not want the responsibilities of a professional qualification and all that would entail in terms of expectations of her. She was adamant that her decision was final. She was referred to the counselling service which she attended very reluctantly. The counsellor recognized that Sheila was unable to make any other decision at that time, and supported her in her decision to leave. If Sheila had been less decisive the counsellor may have been able to work more productively with her.

After the course

Personal tutors may have an important role to play in the life of their students for several years after the end of the course. They may be asked for references, or receive visits or reports from students describing their activities and achievements. Occasionally ex-tutees may ask for an appointment to discuss a concern about their career or educational future. If the relationship has been one of trust and understanding this on-going contact may be rewarding for both student and tutor.

Personal tutor as group facilitator

As student numbers increase, staff–student ratios also increase with the consequence that personal tutorials become very time-consuming. While there are occasions when students want and need individual consultations with their tutors, much personal tutoring can be successfully conducted in a group setting. However to use this approach personal tutors need to feel comfortable with group facilitation skills.

The purpose of group sessions

Earlier in this chapter we have given an outline of student needs and concerns at different points in the academic life-cycle. Group sessions can be held to address any of these issues at different times.

1. Induction: introductions, a discussion of hopes, fears and expectations of the course.
2. Mid first term: settling in, 'how is it?' the good and the bad aspects of university life.
3. Second term: monitoring progress, study skills, preparation for exams.
4. Third term: Coping with exam anxiety, planning revision, thinking about the summer vacation.
5. Second year meetings: Review of year one, life-style, coping strategies for the year, thoughts about the future.
6. Third year meetings: Review of year two, coping strategies for dealing with stress, applying for jobs or placements, career, planning for final examinations, saying goodbye and ending the course.

The advantages for students of meeting in a group setting are many. First, it provides a potential friendship group and a chance to get to know other students. Secondly, when students share their experience with others a normative process occurs, they discover that they are not alone with their anxieties. Thirdly, in a group the whole is more than the sum of the parts and students can gain a sense of feeling included in and belonging to the institution by being part of it.

Ground rules
To function effectively personal tutorial meetings need some ground rules which are usually set by the facilitator and agreed with the students. They should include the following:

• that personal information imparted must be regarded as confidential to the group;
• that students attend the meetings or send apologies if they are unable to do so;
• that everyone should arrive on time, and the meeting ends at the agreed time;
• that one person at a time speaks and others listen;
• that the group exists for the benefit of the students and should be used for discussing issues of their choice.

Setting
The group should be held in a comfortable room without desks in which chairs can be moved to form a circle. The room should be free from interruptions during the sessions. This message can be reinforced by hanging a notice on the door and, if necessary, unplugging the telephone.

Timing of the sessions

It can often be difficult to find a time when the whole group can meet together, however if the personal tutor has access to the timetables of individuals the optimum time can be chosen. Some of the tutors personal tutees may not be able to make that time but it is better to see say twelve students together and then to see a few individually than to abandon the idea of group sessions. Group sessions should be not less than one hour and not more than an hour and a half in duration.

The facilitator

Ideally the group should set its own agenda for the sessions and the personal tutor facilitate this process. All groups are different and some may quickly become active and self-directed whereas others require more encouragement and prompting. For the first few sessions the group facilitator may choose to have some ideas or structures in mind to help the group focus and develop. It is essential not to impose those ideas if the group is able to find its own way. The first part of the strategy should be to ask the students how they want to spend the time. The students may take the group discussion into unexpected territory and it is essential that the tutor has sufficient flexibility to allow the most important issues for the students to emerge.

> *Example:* It was the beginning of the second term of an undergraduate course. The personal tutor had in mind that students might like to think about their progress and study skills. However when the students arrived and she asked if there was anything they would like to talk about, it rapidly emerged that they were concerned about some changes that had been made to the course as a result of a member of staff leaving. There was a lot of strong feeling about the changes and she wisely decided to stay with the students' agenda rather than impose her own.

It is useful for facilitators to ask a few open-ended questions and then sit back and listen to what comes. They may need to help students stick to the ground rules and remind them to listen to one person at a time.

There may be times when the tutor has important information to disseminate to the group, where questions can be asked and discussion can ensue. Space for the thoughts, feelings and concerns raised by the students is also a valuable part of the group process. If the group starts with the facilitator being too directive, or taking up a substantial amount of time talking, it will be difficult to change the focus to the students' active participation.

Exercises

There are many books that give examples of exercises that can be used with groups for a variety of purposes, here we offer an exercise or strategy for a first meeting.

Ask the students to stand up in the middle of the room and choose another student that they do not know very well if at all. Ask them to take two minutes each to introduce themselves to their partner. This might include information about their background, family, interests, likes and dislikes, etc. One should speak and the other listen. At the end of the first two minutes tell them to change listener and speaker roles. Then ask them to sit down with their partner and another pair, and tell them to introduce their partner to the group, with as much detail as they can remember. In that group of four ask them to make a list of their hopes, fears and expectations for their university career. After about ten minutes gather the group together and ask each group of four to report their lists back to the group. You then invite other members of the group to comment on the issues raised by the items on the list. For example, there may be fears such as not being up to the academic demands of the course, or not getting on with flatmates, which may be relevant to several of the people in the group. You can then ask individuals to introduce their original partners to the whole group so that you can begin to put names to faces.

An exercise such as this can help an anxious personal tutor and nervous students get to know each other in a structured and relatively comfortable way. Students can share something of themselves with others and discover that they are not alone with their concerns. Personal tutors can learn about students' expectations of university life and about the motivation and interests of their tutees.

Summary

In this chapter we have considered the role and function of personal tutors and the context in which they work. We have looked at the changing focus of their work at different stages of the academic life cycle. Finally, we have given an outline of how personal tutors might use their precious time creatively and constructively by meeting students in a group setting.

3

Counselling and Listening Skills

All students have problems and concerns, and some of them will choose to discuss these with their personal tutor. They may do so either because they perceive their tutor to be someone who can help them, or because there seems to be no one else they can turn to. At such times personal tutors need to mobilize their helping skills and turn their attention fully onto the student to explore and work towards a resolution of the problem. To some tutors these skills will come relatively easily and a natural rapport develops that is both comforting and constructive for the student. For others the challenge of dealing with personal problems can be daunting taking them into the unfamiliar territory of a student's inner experience.

In this chapter we give an outline of basic counselling and listening skills which a personal tutor can develop and incorporate into their repertoire of helping skills. Although an understanding of this chapter does not transform readers into professional counsellors, ready to tackle all manner of problems that present themselves in depth, it may help them to feel more confident in listening, thinking about, and responding to many scenarios that students are likely to present.

The majority of students have the inner resources to handle their lives, study and relationships but there are times when support, encouragement, clarification or guidance can make the difference between success and failure, manifest as the ability to cope versus being overwhelmed with anxiety, staying on or dropping out. The personal tutor can provide a vital link between the university, the student and the outside world and is the person to whom the student often turns when unsettling change occurs in any of these three dimensions.

When a concern is presented a frequent human response is to placate with reassurance and advice. We tend to avoid pain and anger, often by not acknowledging it, brushing it aside with sympathy or denial. Such responses act as a bar to further exploration therefore inhibiting emotional resolution. The development of counselling skills enables personal tutors to present an alternative response to students' concerns and to help them use their own resources to reach a satisfactory conclusion.

Counselling skills can be used to explore and unravel a student's troubles, to facilitate the identification of needs and to work towards a resolution. Counselling skills should not be confused with advice which may inhibit the capacity to explore underlying issues and foster unhelpful dependency. If someone solves our problems for us we fail to learn from experience. Advice may curtail the consultation and usually prevents further exploration. It is often a quick response to a story that we do not want to hear!

Given that relationships between personal tutors and students are based on mutual respect, trust, understanding and a degree of equality, counselling skills can be used to help students develop independence and autonomy in finding workable solutions to their problems. Tutors also need to be open to students and their dilemmas, whatever they might be, without pre-judgement or prejudice. For example, it is easy to decide that a student is a lazy 'good for nothing' based on past experience and then find it difficult to put aside that view and listen to him when he genuinely wants to make changes and mend his ways.

The skills described in this chapter are intended to help personal tutors enhance their interpersonal communication in tutorial sessions with students. It is, however, of vital importance that tutors recognize the limitations of their skills and training in counselling, and refer students to appropriate professional agencies when the problems presented are beyond their sphere of competence.

The setting

The setting for a tutorial interview can have a considerable effect on the process and outcome of the session. A student is more likely to feel valued and trusting if the space in which the meeting takes place is protected from interruptions at the door or by telephone. A 'Do Not Disturb' sign on the door, perhaps giving a time when you will next be available for appointments or casual callers and switching the telephone through to a secretary creates an atmosphere conveying confidentiality and respect. Two chairs of equal height, at an oblique angle to each other, without the obstruction of a desk or plant will further the cause of putting the student at ease and demonstrating equality. Sitting behind a desk or on chairs of unequal height creates a power relationship that is likely to inhibit self-disclosure.

Tutorials may be arranged at the instigation of tutors or students, sometimes by appointment or in response to a knock at the door. The latter can be problematic for tutors especially when they are engrossed in another activity. It is sometimes appropriate to arrange to meet at a more convenient time when full attention can be given to listening to the student.

The ability to listen

Listening is much more difficult than many people assume. We are all used to dialogue and perhaps academics tend to be more skilled at speaking than listening. There is a natural tendency in conversations to listen for a short while, make connections with our own experience, and then contribute our own thoughts, feelings and experiences on the subject. Active listening involves paying close attention to what is being said, recognizing our own responses, thoughts and feelings, then putting them aside in order to pay attention to the speaker. This process requires the listener to hold on to their temptation to interrupt and to be careful about asking questions or sharing personal experiences. Active listening takes time and patience and comments need to be held until the student has had time to unfold their story. Then verbal acknowledgement that the listener has heard the content, or that some sense has been made of the initial communication, should be given.

There are many blocks to listening of which it is helpful to be aware. For example, if you have something on your mind it is more difficult to concentrate on another person's worries. We often turn off in response to unpalatable material. If the communication is too painful, does not fit with the way we see the world, or impinges too closely on our own concerns, it is more comfortable not to listen.

> *Example:* Sheila was complaining to her male tutor about having been sexually harassed by another member of staff who had asked her to go out with him. The tutor was embarrassed and tried to reassure Sheila that the harassment was not serious.

This is an example of being unable to hear the anger and distress because the issue is uncomfortable and difficult to address. Here the tutor found the allegation against a colleague difficult to believe therefore he denied its serious nature.

Sometimes students do not hear constructive criticism of their work and go on to repeat the same mistakes. Criticism, even when presented in a positive way, can be very threatening to a person with limited self-confidence and the response is often to turn off or listen selectively.

Active listening has a non-verbal element. This involves active participation without words, facilitated by adopting a comfortable and attentive posture, by making eye contact, and by nodding gently in appropriate places to indicate your attention.

Reflection

After listening to the student's initial problem the personal tutor may find it useful to gather the strands together and check that they have correctly interpreted the situation. In other words, to reflect back to the student the gist of what they have said. This kind of reflective response serves several purposes:

1. It tells the student quite conclusively that you have been listening because you give them concrete evidence of what has been heard.

2. It enables the student to correct you if you have missed anything out or if you have misinterpreted a vital piece of information.
3. It enables the student to reflect on what they have said so that they can either move on from there, knowing that you are following closely, or re-evaluate their first statement.

Example:

Student: 'This place is a real dump! The lectures are awful, there are so many students in the lecture theatre at any one time that it is impossible to ask questions or check anything out. I gave in my essay three months ago and it still hasn't been returned. What's more, you should see my room! It's so small you couldn't swing a cat, even if you were allowed to keep one. The walls are so thin that I can hear the person next door breathing. I've a good mind to jack it all in now and get a decent job to earn some money.'

Tutor: 'You're not satisfied with your experience here. You find the lectures unhelpful and you don't think that you are getting enough feedback on the work that you are doing. The final straw is your room and taken together you're having such a bad experience you're considering leaving.'

Student: 'Well I'm not sure I'd go as far as leaving. Now you put it like that maybe it's not quite as bad as it sounds. There are things that really get on my nerves but I've got a lot of good friends here and I suppose I would be very disappointed to leave without a degree. I am a bit surprised by it all though. We had so much more help and attention at school.'

In this example the student is surprised by the force of his own statement and reconsiders his most pressing concerns. The tutor is then able to help him discuss his disappointment and work towards adjusting to his new environment.

Empathy

A vital counselling skill is the use of empathic responses. Empathy involves trying to see an experience as the other person sees it rather than how you see it, in other words, 'putting yourself in their shoes'. Most personal tutors are successful academics whose experience of study has been positive and constructive. In order to help a student who is anxious about examinations or unable to get down to doing any work they need to try and understand the student's perspective on the problem and to communicate their understanding.

Example:

Student: 'I'm really worried about the exams. I've worked so hard and I really want to do well but I'm scared that I will get into that room and my mind will go completely blank, just like it did last year.'

The tutor's response, based on their own experience may be to say, 'Don't worry. Exams are not a problem, You just go in there, relax, and do your best.'

Although the student may feel reassured by this statement it is more likely to induce feelings of irritation because the tutor has not really grasped just how upset and anxious they feel. The problem has been brushed aside with a quick fix bit of advice which neither acknowledges nor addresses the issue.

Alternatively, if the personal tutor tries to imagine what it is like to go blank in an important examination they may be able to make a helpful response based on empathy, such as:

'The prospect of examinations coming up makes you feel anxious, and you fear that you will have the same problem as you had last year. Tell me a bit more about exactly what happens to you.'

The expression of empathy is another way of showing that you are listening and understanding at a deeper level than non-verbal listening and reflection convey. Making empathic comments will have a profound effect on the interaction between tutor and tutee and sometimes such comments will appropriately provoke an emotional response.

Example:
Student: 'I haven't really been able to get myself back into gear since my mum died. Everyone's been very good, and I've caught up on all the notes, but I can't really concentrate to write an essay. I keep thinking about her all the time (spoken with tears in her eyes).'
Tutor: 'You're still very upset about you mother's death. You probably will be for quite a while. It's understandable that you are having difficulty keeping up with work under the circumstances.'

In this interaction the tutor did not dodge the emotional content of the student's statement, instead he was able to empathize with her by directly addressing the student's distress. He allowed her to cry and did not rush to reassure her or divert her away from her feelings.

Sometimes it will not be obvious from the spoken word what the student is feeling during an interview. The tutor may have an intuitive hunch about what is going on and, at the right moment, may tentatively try it out.

Example: Rachel was a final year student talking about her doubts concerning her future career. The tutor knew that she had always had her mind firmly set on a particular avenue, and her current worries did not seem to fit. There was a piece missing in the jigsaw. He played his hunch by saying, 'I can see that you have some concerns about how life will be when you start your new job, but I have been wondering whether you might also be feeling a bit upset about leaving here. You've made a lot of friends and it is hard to say goodbye.'
Rachel: (Looking upset). 'You're right, I don't want to say goodbye.'

Open-ended questions

So far reflective responses have been described which are appropriate to use throughout an interview. Questions tend to come to the listener more spontaneously than reflective or empathic statements. Questions are necessary at times although a successive string without other forms of intervention can be more like an interrogation and should be avoided. Open-ended questions are most helpful because they can help people begin to talk.

An open-ended question is one which elicits more than a yes/no or other one-word answer. It invites the student to open up or elaborate on a particular point, to expand the picture rather than narrowing it down. The type of questions that may be useful in a tutorial interview include the following:

- How is the course going?
- How do you feel about what is happening?
- How do you get on with the other students?
- What would you like to change?
- What courses of action have you thought about so far?
- What do the others think?
- Tell me more about . . .
- How do you imagine I can help you . . .

Although 'Why' questions are open-ended it is wise to use them sparingly because they can be interpreted as persecutory. 'Why' questions are often used in disciplinary circumstances for instance 'Why did you do that?' If people knew why things happened or why they did things in a particular way, they wouldn't need to ask for help!

It is also possible to re-frame questions and instead make a tentative empathic statement. Leading phrases such as 'I guess' or 'I am wondering' or 'I am thinking that' can be used to formulate and communicate your hunch, insight or understanding.

Example:
Student: 'I don't like it here and I don't think I will be able to stay.'

Instead of a question such as 'What is it you don't like?' the tutor could respond with something like, 'I guess is has been hard for you to settle down in this new environment.'

Example:
Student: 'I can't keep up with the work. I am two assignments behind, and I can't seem to find the time to do them.'

Rather than asking 'What do you do with your time?' the tutor who has some prior knowledge of the student might say, 'I wonder whether your commitments to the students union have anything to do with your time problem.'

The use of summarizing

The use of counselling skills does not come easily to everyone and it is not uncommon to get to a certain point using the skills above then feel stuck. This is often the time to summarize. The summary should clarify what has been said and give an overview of the problem presented. This is helpful to the tutor as it gives them an opportunity to think aloud. The student can correct any wrong assumptions and begin to look at the problem more objectively. The summary lays all the cards on the table for review from a new perspective. Particular issues or aspects can then be picked up for further scrutiny.

Changing the picture

When the tutor has listened intently to the student's story, communicated empathy and understanding, and perhaps summarized what has been said, it may be time to move on to the next phase of counselling. This often feels more comfortable and familiar to tutors as it involves looking for possible solutions. A useful question to ask at this stage is, 'What would have to happen in order for you to feel better about this situation?' What this question does is to take the student from the present scenario into the future and ask them to begin to think about possible avenues that may lead to an ultimate solution to their problem.

> *Example:* Stuart has been telling you about all the genuine and dis-
> tressing reasons why he has fallen behind with his work. You have
> listened carefully, expressed concern and understanding, recogni-
> zed and acknowledged the distress he feels about his mother's illness
> and summarized the current scenario. You ask Stuart a question simi-
> lar to that given above, and he pauses to reflect on the answer. He
> then says,

> > 'I suppose that I shall begin to feel better when my life is back
> > in some kind of routine. I need to make a start with getting my
> > notes in order and tackling one of the outstanding essays. I'll
> > have to do some planning. Also I'm more settled now that my
> > mother is well but I would like to spend a bit of time with her.
> > It might help if I went home for a week because I can work
> > better there.'

> At this point you would be able to assist Stuart in weighing up the
> advantages and disadvantages of possible courses of action and sub-
> sequently help him to make an action plan. Giving him a further
> appointment will provide him with a time boundary to work towards
> and an opportunity to monitor his progress.

Confrontation

Inviting a student to think about what needs to happen in order to make things change is one form of gentle confrontation. Being able to tactfully confront students with their behaviour or its consequences is an essential counselling skill. Sometimes a tutorial will begin on this note, particularly if the student has been summoned by the tutor. If this is the case it is important to be clear about the issue to be raised and to present the evidence or information as concisely and honestly as possible.

Example: Robert's tutor asked to see him when he heard that Robert had been told to leave his hall of residence after a drunken night of parties and vandalism. He started the interview like this:

'Robert, I heard about the incident last week at the Hall of Residence. I feel concerned about what happened and I imagine that you might be feeling quite distressed about it too, particularly now that you have been asked to leave your accommodation. Could you tell me a bit about what happened and particularly what your part in it all was.'

Robert told his story and acknowledged that he had had far too much to drink. His tutor picked that up and confronted him again:

'I wonder if it is time to stop and think about whether you have a drink problem and if so to take steps to deal with it?'

Such a confrontation, although tentative, can be very powerful. The problem may be denied at the time but often people go away and think about what has been said and take action later.

Sometimes a confrontation is needed during a tutorial/counselling session.

Example: Samantha was giving a whole list of excuses to explain why her assignments were always late. Her tutor was sympathetic up to a point but felt increasingly that Samantha was not taking responsibility for herself or her actions and said,

'Samantha, I appreciate that a lot of things have happened to disrupt you, but perhaps you need to think a bit more about your part in all of this. What steps do you need to take to stay more in control of your environment?'

Another time when a confronting statement can be appropriate is when non-verbal behaviour is not congruent with what is said.

Example: Ted was telling his tutor how happy he was at university and how pleased he was to have chosen the place and the course. As he was speaking he sighed frequently and looked quite miserable and lifeless. The tutor said:

'I hear you telling me that all is well but you look miserable, and I am wondering if things are quite as rosy as you paint them.'

At this Ted looked up, sighed again, and revealed that he was taking a subject because his parents wanted him to, it was not his personal choice.

Although confrontation sounds harsh it can be done in a tentative, supportive and gentle way. The most important principles are sensitively to confront one issue at a time and to be prepared to listen carefully to the response.

Reflective thinking

During a personal tutorial both the tutor and student may need to pause from time to time to think about what has been discussed, not necessarily to search for solutions, rather to consider the underlying meaning and context of the problem. It can be helpful for the tutor to allow silences in the communication from time to time. When a space or silence occurs at an appropriate moment it puts pressure on the student to reflect on their situation, which sometimes leads to deeper insight and creativity. Alternatively, if the student fills every moment of the session with verbal discourse leaving no pause for thought, the tutor can intervene by saying something like, 'Let's just sit back for a minute and think about what you have been saying.'

People have all kinds of defence mechanisms that protect them from uncomfortable thoughts and feelings. One such mechanism is to fill up time and space with speech or activity so that there is no time for experiencing anything painful or disturbing. Inviting someone to sit back and think or reflect can in some instances have a powerful effect.

Self-disclosure

A counselling tutorial session is different from a normal conversation, when we usually share things about ourselves, in that the focus should be on the student and their concerns. If we start talking about our own experience, we take the attention from the student and stop listening. Our life experiences may be similar to those being recounted but they are never the same as someone else's and it is unwise to assume that they are.

Personal tutors may at times draw on their own experience to inform their thinking and understanding which helps them make an empathic response to a student, but it is usually inappropriate to share their actual experience.

Example: Flora told her tutor how upset she was about her parents' divorce. The tutor's parents had also divorced when she was a similar age to Flora, and she remembered how upset and confused she had been. The tutor was able to respond with empathy to Flora's feelings of guilt and her sense of responsibility for the break up which enabled Flora to explore her feelings in considerable depth.

In this instance the tutor's personal experience enabled her to help her tutee work through her feelings and eventually come to terms with her parents' separation. It was not necessary for the tutor to disclose her own family troubles.

Brain storming

Another way of opening up ideas and possibilities is by brain storming, or encouraging the student to generate a range of options or possibilities, including negative ones.

> *Example:* Louise was unhappy with her accommodation. As her personal tutor listened carefully to her concerns the trust between them grew. Louise eventually divulged the fact that her flat mates were heavy drug users, that she was finding it difficult to resist their invitations to join in with them and that she was feeling increasingly isolated.
>
> Although sorely tempted to be judgemental of the flat mates and rush in with good advice the tutor restrained himself and asked her to generate a list of options for the possible ways forward. In reply Louise said:
>
> 'I suppose that I should look around for another flat, I could go to the accommodation office to see if they have anything to offer. I do worry about my friends though, they are getting worse and worse. I could try and tackle them but that would be difficult. I have thought about leaving altogether and going home to get a job. Or I could just do nothing and stick it out until the end of the year.'

Evaluating the options

In this instance, having generated some ideas, the tutor helped the student to move on to evaluate the possibilities by looking at the factors for and against them. People often feel stuck and powerless and it is important to include an evaluation of the consequences of taking no action.

In the case of Louise there are two aspects of the problem to consider; first, what she does to take care of herself and secondly, how she manages her concern for her friends. In this case it is important to encourage her to put her own needs before those of her friends and to help her to make an action plan to protect herself. She also needs time to consider her

friends. She may have feelings of loss at leaving them or of guilt and responsibility for their welfare if she cannot find a way of helping them.

Action plan

It is helpful to go through an action plan with the student at the end of a
meeting so that they can leave with as much clarity as possible about their
future choices. The tutor might help students to consider the details of an
action plan such as when, how, with whom, at what cost, in what way, and
so on. The most important thing may be to offer another appointment after
a suitable time interval to follow up on their action.

Variations on this sequence of counselling skills

The counselling skills used by the tutor should respond to the needs of the
student. For example if the student has suffered a bereavement, is upset, or
finding it difficult to adjust the most helpful response of the tutor is often
to listen and empathize. The student will take time to come to terms with
their loss and readjust to their new circumstances. The attention, care and
concern of the tutor together with time to reflect on the past and ponder
on the future often is in itself therapeutic. There may be times when it is
helpful to respond differently. For example, if the tutor feels that the student is in need of more help than they are able to give they may suggest
referral to the counsellor or chaplain. Alternatively, the time will come
when a bereaved student may need help to formulate an action plan for
getting back to work.

Coping with feelings

An effective listener is able to tolerate the expression of strong feelings
without distracting the student from them. It is a common aspect of British
culture to turn away from feelings. A familiar mode of dealing with sadness
is by using reassurance, telling the student that 'it doesn't really hurt', or
'there there never mind', effectively denying their painful experience. If
someone is upset it is not unusual for the listener to suggest making a cup
of tea. Such provision can be comforting and therapeutic as long as it is
not used to escape from the emotion being expressed. Making the tea is
an action that denotes caring, particularly if the listener is lost for words
to find a response.

Tolerating the feelings of another person can be difficult because they
resonate with uncomfortable feelings in the listener.

Example: Adam was talking to his tutor about the pain and guilt he
was experiencing after the termination of his girlfriend's pregnancy.

The tutor was very moved by the student's expression of feeling and became aware of his own sadness about his wife's recent miscarriage. He felt uncomfortable and because of this directed the interview towards the consideration of practical work related matters with the student rather hastily.

It is difficult to empathize with a student if the tutor identifies too closely with their concern and in these circumstances it is prudent to refer the student on to someone else to discuss that particular issue. Alternatively, a further appointment could be arranged a few days later and, in the meantime, the tutor could seek an opportunity to discuss his difficult feelings with someone else, for instance a counsellor, so that the next time they meet he is more able to tune into the student's distress.

Counselling skills in a personal tutoring context

The counselling skills described here are those which we consider to be appropriate for a personal tutor to use and which can be relatively easily acquired or refined through reading and practice or at a short counselling skills or personal tutoring workshop. These skills are powerful and valuable to use in the tutorial context but do not constitute counselling training. It is important that personal tutors recognize their strengths and weaknesses in tackling student problems and make clear decisions about their level of competence related to each problem presented by a student. There are no hard and fast rules as people and situations are different and must be given specific consideration. For example let us consider two students who experience a bereavement:

> *Example:* Angela's mother died of cancer. Angela was very upset and took two weeks off from her studies. She returned to university and made an appointment to see her tutor. She expressed a lot of her feelings and concerns to the tutor, who was able to listen and be understanding. Angela had had a good relationship with her mother and, although she was distressed by her loss, she seemed to be experiencing a normal bereavement process. Her tutor felt that he could be supportive of Angela as she went through this painful life experience.

> *Example:* Jonathan's brother was killed in a motorcycle accident. He returned to college after the funeral and contacted his tutor a few weeks later. Jonathan reported that he was unable to concentrate, was not sleeping, and was drinking excessively to try to make himself sleep. It transpired that Jonathan felt responsible for his brother's death because he had been the more successful of the pair. The tutor in this instance correctly recognized that Jonathan was finding it difficult to work through the bereavement and wisely referred him to the counselling service for more specialist help.

In these examples the tutors involved assessed the nature of the students' problems and decided on their level of competence to deal with them. Angela's tutor recognized that he could help her process her bereavement, whereas Jonathan's tutor felt out of his depth and suggested professional counselling.

The hidden agenda

If a student has a problem that they are ashamed of or embarrassed about it is not easy to present it to their personal tutor even though they may wish to talk about it. In this instance students often open an interview by presenting a different, safer issue, to test the water. The tutor needs to keep an open mind about whether the first issue presented is the most important one and to be alert to the hidden agenda. It is important to listen carefully and it can sometimes be useful to reflect back what the student has said, adding 'and have you any other difficulties?' If the student gains confidence that the tutor is listening to and taking seriously their concerns the underlying problem is given space to emerge. A common opening statement might be concern about being on the wrong course, or at the wrong college.

> *Example:* Susan asked to see her tutor to discuss changing her options. She spent fifteen minutes talking about how she was bored with her subjects and that she had changed her mind about her future career. The tutor sensed that there was more to this problem as Susan had always been very committed to her subject, and eventually asked if anything else was bothering her. At this point Susan burst into tears and told him that a relationship she had been having with another student on the course had recently ended and that she was finding it too painful to see him every day in lectures.

In this case it would have been easy to continue along the wrong path of discussing careers and subjects rather than dealing with the real issues of loss and pain.

Changing course or college

Some students decide for many different reasons to change their course or college. Some of these cases are quite straightforward. They have received poor career guidance at school, have been pressurized by parents into a particular course, or have accepted a last minute clearing house place in a subject that was not their preference. However a request to change may be the tip of the iceberg, as shown in the foregoing example. These decisions sometimes represent a young person's attempt to gain control of their environment when they do not feel in control of their internal world. For some leaving home and going away to college is a welcome relief from parental control, for which they are well prepared. For others this can be a profound shock that hurtles them unexpectedly into a confrontation with their independent existence and isolation. A closer look at the request to change course may disclose separation anxiety, especially if a student wishes to return home, or a crisis of adjustment.

In this instance careful counselling that considers and explores the presenting problem rather than rushed decisions can be of enormous benefit to the student. It may allow them to make an informed choice rather than take an impulsive course of action. For some the problem is too severe for them to stay and work at it. The level of anxiety about being away from home is such that they are unable to tolerate anything other than instant relief. For others by giving support to the 'adult' part of them that recognizes that they have a problem the tutor may be able to help them to take care of their 'child' part. The tutor may be able to provide sufficient support for the student if there is a good working relationship and time to see them regularly, or the decision may be taken to refer them to the counselling service. It is important to note that for students referred for specialist help continued contact with their tutor can be a vital adjunct to the therapy.

The other side of this is to watch out for students who have transferred from other colleges or courses, and be alert to whatever has caused them to move. This may have solved the problem in the short term, for instance being nearer to home, or they may have brought it with them. The tutor's interest and sensitivity towards them may make all the difference to the stressful process of settling into a new environment.

> *Example:* Norma had transferred from another university to do the same course for personal reasons she did not wish to discuss. Her tutor respected her wish not to discuss the matter but decided to make a point of seeing her regularly for the first few months. Norma found it more difficult to integrate than she thought she would, the course was different in some respects to the one she had left and the other students had already formed friendship groups. She became depressed and confided in her tutor that after two months she was feeling just as bad as she had at her previous university. He recognized that her problem was not with the course or the subject but was related to her internal world. She was disillusioned and depressed and the tutor referred her to the counselling service.

Swinging the lead

Contrary to the beliefs of many students, colleges and universities have no investment in seeing students fail and will usually do everything possible, other than lowering academic standards, to ensure that students are treated fairly. One of the ways in which leniency is demonstrated is by taking into account personal circumstances that may have impeded performance such as illness, death of a relative or other traumatic incident. Most students who appeal to their personal tutors for help due to extraordinary circumstances are genuine. There will be others who ask for no help, but who the tutor knows to have had difficulties. However there will always be one or two students who attempt to use this aspect of the system to their advantage.

Example: Gavin visited his tutor just after examinations to say that he felt he had not done very well and he wanted to explain why. The tutor was interested in the reasons he gave. Gavin had been social secretary for the Guild of Students, which had taken up most of his time during the second year of his course. He had enjoyed it and the experience would help him with his future career in the music industry, however during that year his academic work had been secondary in importance. The tutor was sympathetic with Gavin's feelings of regret but put the responsibility for his time and work management firmly back with Gavin. At this point Gavin played his last card which was that he had been very upset about the death of his grandmother the previous November, and he explained that this had stopped him working.

In this example the story about grandmother was probably true but Gavin had left it very late in the year to come and discuss it. He had also already admitted that he had been absorbed elsewhere. It seemed to the tutor that Gavin was 'swinging the lead' by trying to get the system to make allowances for him even though his problems were largely of his own making. His tutor offered to help him with time planning and self-management during the following year which Gavin was asked to repeat. He did not pursue the tutor's offer.

Coping with failures and counselling out

Despite a largely benevolent system some students do not make it. Many colleges allow endless re-sits that students repeatedly fail. It may befall the personal tutor the unenviable task of suggesting that the time has come to leave. This kind of confrontation is not easy because the tutor is facing the student with an aspect of reality that is difficult to accept. The anxieties students experience are not only about academic achievement and career, they are also about their attachment to the institution. For some clinging onto a college or course defends them against adulthood and independence. It is helpful to anticipate the student's emotional response which is likely to include pain, anger and disappointment, and to give space to enable the student to talk about the future and to make plans. It is also important to listen to the words between the lines, to recognize personal development as well as practical issues. Referral to a counsellor may be appropriate.

On courses leading to vocational qualifications it occasionally becomes clear to the course team that a certain student is unsuitable for the profession for which they are training. To add to the problem these are often students who are unable to hear or use feedback, and hence who are resistant to change and have to be 'counselled out'. As they have not heard feedback about their performance all along, they are unlikely to hear it now. They cannot accept even sensitively framed comments about their unsuitability and often accuse the tutor of persecuting them. Sometimes such students threaten legal action and invoke the complaints procedure by their actions reinforcing the initial impression that this person is unable to cope with feedback, which impedes their learning.

Techniques and interventions which may be suitable in this instance include the following:

- being very clear about rules, regulations and procedure and following them to the letter;
- speaking clearly and precisely when giving feedback;
- documenting every communication in full, recording conversations as accurately as possible;
- being calm and empathic at all times. Recognizing the distress that the incident has caused and the student's anger;
- being firm and unwavering on the decision made to exclude the student;
- ensuring the student is aware that the decision has been made at exam board level, the tutor is not personally responsible and is therefore able to pick up some of the pieces.

Challenging problems presented by students

Some student problems pose difficult challenges to the personal tutor. Here we outline some examples.

The silent type

Students are not always good communicators. This may be for any one of many reasons including personality type, lack of confidence, deference to an authority figure, or anxiety about revealing personal concerns. A familiar encounter might be with a student who appears for their personal tutorial session then says little or nothing. The tutor feels uncomfortable and pressurized to keep the conversation going.

Several things are important in this interview. First, to recognize that the student has the right to be silent if they so choose. Secondly, to be clear with the student about the purpose of the interview. Thirdly, to be careful to use open ended questions that provide opportunities for the student to reflect on their experience and by avoiding a sequence of closed questions as this sets up an interrogation style of interview. It may also be appropriate to use a tentative empathic enquiry or comment at some stage, acknowledging the anxiety that the interview induces, such as:

'I'm imagining that you might be feeling uncomfortable or anxious about sitting here talking to me. Perhaps you are concerned about the confidentiality of this interview and the implications for your assessment.'

Such a comment or question demonstrates that you are trying to see the world, or the interview in this case, as the other person sees it. It may increase the trust between you, or fall on stony ground. Finally, at the end of the session, it is often helpful to state that the student is welcome to come and speak to the tutor again. It is not unusual for students to test the water with their tutors on one occasion and to return sometime later to talk about their more profound concerns.

The independent type

Some students have no problem coping with and being successful in their college experience. They are independent, confident, clear about their objectives and abilities and able to organize their time and their lives. Others appear independent, act as though they have life taped, then fall flat on their faces.

Students in both these groups often do not attend their personal tutorials. The first group will survive whereas the second type may not. One of the symptoms of this second group can best be described by considering project work. The determined independent student could produce a project with no reference whatsoever to the project supervisor. They present it confidently on the prescribed date and are then horrified to be told that it is not what was asked for, that the methodology was wrong or that the standard falls far short of that required. Had the student consulted the supervisor this problem may have been avoided.

Unless there is a very rigid personal tutorial system that requires students to attend tutorial sessions and penalizes them if they do not it is unlikely that the personal tutor will meet these 'independent' students until it is too late. This poses a dilemma for the tutor, who is pushed into a position from which it is often impossible to help the student.

It may be useful to consider what has caused this student to behave in this way. Perhaps they have had independence forced upon them from an early age, with a lack of constructive and supportive parental guidance. Rather than trusting adults to be non-judgemental they have looked within themselves for answers and directions. An immediate response to someone who has come unstuck because of their reluctance to ask for help, might be one of 'I told you so' or 'It's all your own fault', which is both judgemental and critical, exactly the type of response that the self-determined behaviour had sought to avoid. An alternative more supportive and constructive response such as, 'Let's see how we can best help you to deal with this problem' could be one step towards helping the student to develop trust and confidence in authority figures.

The help-rejecting complainer

Once in a while personal tutors will come across a 'help-rejecting complainer'. This is a student who has a thousand and one problems for which there are no solutions, whose most common response begins with 'Yes, but . . .' It is the type of student most likely to send the personal tutor scurrying into someone else's office when they are seen approaching. In order to help such a student it is useful to have some insight into the workings of their mind. Ultimately the problem is an expression of resentful dependence, an abdication of personal responsibility. In their encounter with the tutor they are effectively saying that they cannot take care of them-selves and are finding it difficult to get a grip on the world. They want help but it is never quite right when offered. This often happens when a student has an idealized view of how life should be, and cannot therefore tolerate the disappointment when it fails to match up to their expectations. They will seek far and wide, possibly approaching all the helping agencies, to find the answer that will put the picture straight and enable them to hold onto their idealized fantasy.

The personal tutor of this student is only one port of call. When dealing with such a student it is useful to recognize that however hard you try to assist them you are likely to fail, because the student is unable to accept help. The conscientious and caring personal tutor may spend many unfruitful hours with such students, resulting in guilt and despair when nothing improves.

Once a help-rejecting complainer has been identified the personal tutor would be wise to consult the counselling service. A typical outcome of inter-action with such a student is that the tutor will worry about the student's expressed problem, taking it on board as if it were their own. This leaves the student temporarily relieved of the burden. The counsellor may be able to recognize this, give the tutor some understanding of the dynamics of the interaction, and subsequently help the student, although it may be a long term process.

> *Example:* George was a final year student struggling with his Engineer-ing project. He consulted his tutor several times to ask for help. The tutor gave him relevant references and helped him by talking through the structure of the project. The tutor was amazed when a colleague mentioned to him a few days later that he had also seen George and had also offered some help with the project. When the project was submitted some time later it was clear that George had not followed the guidelines offered to him and the project was referred. George was furious and made an official complaint about the lack of help and support he had received. His tutor confronted him with the fact that he had had considerably more help than most other students, men-tioning also George's disappointment and anger at failing the project.

Help-rejecting complainers are difficult people to deal with. It is some-times appropriate to confront them with their disappointment that life is not all that they would wish although ultimately the tutor may have to accept that such students are not amenable to help.

Suicidal threats

There are all kinds of myths and misinformation circulating about the type of people who commit suicide. Adolescence is a period of development characterized by vulnerability when young people are prone to depression, mood swings and occasionally to brief psychotic episodes. This is enlarged in Chapter 4. During adolescence thoughts of suicide are common. Other transitional periods, such as mid-life, bring with them developmental crises of a similar nature (explored further in Chapter 6).

When suicidal thoughts, threats or plans are conveyed to the personal tutor they should always be taken seriously. Sometimes, if the words are not specifically used but the implication is there, it is wise to ask sensitively whether the student has ever considered suicide, so that the issue is brought into the open rather than circumvented. When there is evidence of suicidal intention it is also essential that the student is advised to see their general practitioner. In parallel with this it is also helpful to continue regular meetings, to support them through a difficult period of time.

There are not many circumstances in which we advocate advice however in this instance it is essential not only for the welfare of the student but also for the protection of the tutor. Most people who mention suicide take no action but those who do have usually talked about the possibility beforehand. Referring the student to their GP has several implications. First, it informs the student that the tutor has heard and understood their concerns and taken them seriously. This encourages them to view themselves more seriously and take action to get help. Secondly, it conveys care and concern, especially important if they are feeling depressed and unloved. Lastly, it gives professional cover in that the tutor has taken every possible action to help the student.

We have written earlier about the importance of confidentiality in the tutorial role. On occasions when life is at risk confidentiality cannot be guaranteed. The personal tutor should in the first instance make every effort to encourage the student to see their GP, however if they refuse the tutor should inform the student that they will have to speak to the GP, because they cannot carry the burden of confidentiality given the potential consequences of the student's actions.

Some people commit suicide without hinting to anyone that it is a possibility and no one is aware of their inner distress. Sometimes suicide is the result of a psychotic episode or the use of drugs or alcohol. In the event of the suicide of a personal tutee, particularly one well known to the tutor, it may be very valuable for the tutor to seek an interview with a counsellor. This can provide an opportunity to share emotional trauma, review the tutor's actions and perhaps to learn from mistakes. Similarly, in the aftermath of a suicide the other casualties are the deceased's friends and colleagues. For them an invitation to talk may be appreciated.

Sexuality

Exploration of sexual identity is a crucial part of adolescent development as described in Chapter 4 and aspects of sexuality may present themselves in personal tutorials. For instance students may use their personal tutorial sessions to take steps towards recognition and acknowledgement of their homosexuality. Students may disclose information about pregnancy, abortion, psychosexual problems, being HIV positive or having Aids. Any of these may be unfamiliar territory for the personal tutor and in dealing with such disclosures it is essential to avoid statements of judgement and direct advice. Students want to talk through these anxieties with an understanding and sympathetic listener.

When tutors have strongly held beliefs which may prevent them from giving unbiased attention to students, they should consider referring them elsewhere. For instance if a pregnant student wants advice about termination their needs may not be best served by a devout Roman Catholic tutor whose allegiance to the Pope may interfere with their capacity to put the students needs first.

There may be occasions when a student behaves in a flirtatious way towards a tutor, which can be exciting or uncomfortable. The student may be telling you through their behaviour something about how they deal with authority. Their sexual overtures may be a defence against feeling vulnerable and dependent, a smoke screen hiding their more childlike needs. It may be a reflection of immaturity rather than adulthood, an expression of a wish to charm or gain favour with a parental figure. The tutor's response to sexual overtures is important. It is essential to avoid the trap of falling into a sexual relationship with a vulnerable student where there is a marked imbalance of power, as this constitutes a form of sexual abuse. In such instances the tutor may be liable to allegations of sexual harassment.

Referral

We have discussed some potentially serious student problems in this chapter particularly relating to suicide and sexuality and have often said that students may need to be referred to another agency. Referral is an important skill in itself and needs to be handled with care. The most important aspects of referral are to ensure that students know:

- why they are being referred to someone else;
- what they can expect from the person or agency to whom they are being referred;
- that the relationship with the tutor will continue.

It may be clear to the personal tutor that a student has a problem that they cannot help with, but this may not be clear to the student until they are confronted with it.

Example: There had been a lot of complaints about Daniel's behaviour during lectures and seminars. He made aggressive and sometimes abusive comments to others and had alienated himself from his seminar group. His tutor was informed of the problem by other staff and a tutorial was arranged. This aimed to be supportive rather than disciplinary. The meeting started with a general chat then the tutor confronted Daniel with the problem he had been told about. In response Daniel became aggressive and denied that there was a problem.

In this case the tutor has to consider how best to handle Daniel. He might be tempted to refer him to the counsellor, having decided that it was too much for him to handle. The result may be either that Daniel would not keep his appointment or that he would turn up to see the counsellor saying that he had been sent and did not know why. If he responds in this way it indicates that he does not accept responsibility for the problem, in which case he is unlikely to sort it out.

On the other hand, the tutor could exercise his patience and skills to help Daniel recognize the impact he has on others which may involve all or any of the following:

• acknowledging Daniel's anger and irritation at being confronted with the problem;
• recognizing the embarrassment he may feel at this being noticed;
• recognizing his right to stay as he is;
• gently confronting Daniel with the consequences of continuing to behave in the same way, particularly his isolation;
• trying to empathize in order to try and understand why he behaves in this way;
• working towards helping Daniel to acknowledge that he has a problem, without implying criticism or judgement;
• explaining the work of the counselling service including details such as confidentiality;
• giving Daniel the responsibility of contacting the service rather than doing it for him;
• arranging to see Daniel again in a week's time for a review;
• recognizing that it may take a while before Daniel feels ready to contact a counsellor and that he may prefer to talk to the personal tutor a few more times before he makes that decision.

Summary

In this chapter we have given an overview of the basic listening and counselling skills that will assist a personal tutor in their work. We have referred to specific instances such as potential suicide or transfer from another college or course, which may require additional help. We have given illustrations of certain types of students who may demand the attention of the tutor, to whom a cautious response is recommended. Reading about skills may in itself be helpful. If the tutor is also in a position to attend a brief course in personal tutoring or counselling skills this can provide an invaluable adjunct to their role as personal tutor. We would highly recommend this course of action.

4

Adolescence

The majority of students in higher education enter as school leavers. They are usually eighteen or nineteen years of age and in the mid to late stages of adolescent development. In this chapter we will present an outline of this developmental process and the problems it engenders. Emphasis will be placed on the interaction of adolescence with higher education through the exploration of problems encountered by tutors.

Adolescence is a period of transition between childhood and adulthood. This process does not develop in a sequential, logical manner but instead is dynamic. This means that the individual takes two steps forward, one back, one forward, one back, and so on, oscillating between a childlike and adult state. Over a period of time the child state is gradually left behind and a more adult role is adopted. People face the challenges of this developmental process in an individual style at their own pace. This means it is not possible to describe adolescence in absolute terms, with a finite start and end point.

Adolescence is customarily divided into three phases, early, mid, and late. In recent years puberty, usually taken as the starting point of adolescence, has shifted forward and now probably commences for many children at the age of ten or eleven. The end stages tend to be more gradual and hence harder to define, but many authors describe adolescence continuing until at least the age of twenty-five.

Physical changes

The beginning of adolescence is marked by physical changes which consist of a rapid growth spurt and puberty. The pace of growth can be startling to the observer and also to the person undergoing it. In parallel the early development of adult sexual organs begins. External physical changes are dramatic, but internally psychological development occurs at a different pace, the result can be conflict and confusion.

Example: Ruth was eighteen but depending how she dressed could appear to be twelve or twenty-five. She enjoyed being 'grown up' some of the time but also needed to be a little girl. For instance she was proud of the fact she could both pass for a child, obtaining reduced admission, or an adult when she went to the cinema. Her tutor found her difficult to relate to because of the variety of personae she displayed.

Example: George was eighteen and a late developer. This caused difficulties, he was self-conscious about his appearance and embarrassed when asked to prove his age in bars. In tutorials he was quiet and appeared to lack confidence. In a personal tutorial he confided that he was worried about relating to girls, he felt his youthful looks hindered his heterosexual relationships.

Ruth and George were at opposite ends of a developmental continuum and both experienced frustrations which related to their physical and psychological maturation being out of step. Neither looked their chronological age and this became a problem when they came in contact with outsiders who based their expectations on first impressions. To some extent this was compounded by the attitudes of parents, teachers, and members of their peer groups who also struggled with apparent discrepancies.

Ruth and George represent extreme examples of a common adolescent dilemma, namely whether to be an adult or a child. There are advantages and disadvantages to both positions. Adulthood represents freedom, independence, and responsibility for taking care of oneself. Childhood is associated with play, growth, and being nurtured and protected by others on whom one is heavily dependent. Both are attractive but for different and conflicting reasons.

Psychological development

Rapid physical growth tends to slow in the mid phase of adolescence while pubescent changes continue. Alongside this the individual begins to look more like the adult they will eventually become. One of the major psychological developmental changes is increasingly manifest, the struggle to establish an adult identity. This may appear as rebelliousness, the young person refusing to take on the values and attitudes of their parents and teachers, instead constantly questioning principles and at times ignoring advice and instructions.

Example: Peter handed in an essay two days late on three consecutive occasions. His tutor spoke to him to try to discover why. Peter could not say, but went on to talk about his strict upbringing and described the immense sense of relief he had experienced on moving out of his parental home. His parents would constantly nag him about homework, even at the age of eighteen when Peter felt ready to take responsibility for himself.

Once Peter started to talk about his parents he realized just how angry he was at the way they had belittled him. He also recognized that his late assignments were a protest against the course tutors who, being people in authority, represented his parents. By his actions Peter was symbolically rebelling against his strict and rigid parents and in so doing trying to establish his own sense of identity. As often happens he initially overstated the case in his determination not to emulate his parents. In the course of time he found a happier, intermediate position which was more fitting for him.

There are healthy aspects contained within rebellion. When a young person does not question or challenge authority in any shape or form this is often the result of a poor sense of personal worth and identity with correspondingly low self-esteem.

> *Example:* During a tutorial Roger mentioned his feelings of depression. He was clearly very low in spirits and said he had been like this on and off since the age of thirteen. He was a quiet, shy individual with few friends. The tutor had previously noticed that he seldom spoke in class discussions. When Roger did make a contribution it was usually in the form of a quotation, he rarely expressed an opinion or got involved in even the most mildly heated debate.

Roger's depression was linked to his low self-esteem. He felt so worthless he was certain no one would want to hear what he thought about either his academic subject or himself. He had not yet entered a period of adolescent rebellion. He was referred to the counselling service where he was able to explore his feelings about himself and as a result, over the course of a few months, gradually learned to value himself more. He began to participate actively in debates and his depressive symptoms slowly resolved. It seemed that he had been squashing down his personality so effectively he had almost ceased to exist.

Alienation and isolation

Alienation and fear of rejection are common adolescent worries particularly in the middle and late phases. In early adolescence dependency is expressed mainly towards parent figures. In moving from the position of child to adult dependency is transferred from parents to peer group. Roger was heavily dependent on his parents and his self-esteem was closely linked to his wish to please them. He felt that if he failed to do this he would be rejected and ultimately become isolated, unloved and alone in the world. In turn this overdependence on his parents made it difficult for him to become fully integrated with his peers thus he became alienated from them. The balance was not working in his favour. He belonged with neither his parents nor his peers, which reinforced both his feelings of failure and depression.

Peer groups

Like-minded groups are part of our natural social structures. They are diverse in form and can be based on mutual interests, such as music or architecture. Alternatively, they may revolve around the workplace or college, or be set up according to age bands. Adolescent peer groups are a particular type of social group in which the members are bound together by the shared experience of this stage of life. These groups provide an important teething ground for the budding adult and can have both positive and negative influences on development.

Sharing adversity tends to bring people closer, they are more easily able to empathize and so can offer support, understanding, and care to each other. Young people in the early stages of identity formation are able to take on a group identity which can form a safe temporary haven and ultimately strengthen individual development. Instead of launching an individual protest against the unfairness of life, adolescents often protest en masse. This usually involves adopting a visible culture, or uniform, which both separates them from the rest of society and joins them together as a group. This process is an important part of adolescent development, however as with any collective statement the individual has to make compromises to fit in to the norms of the group, and in some instances this process of conformity can be dangerous.

Example: Greg came to a seminar with his sleeves rolled up and numerous circular infected scabs on his forearms. On a pretext his tutor arranged to see him afterwards and enquired about his health. Greg said he was fine, no problems at all thank you. The tutor then asked directly what had happened to his arms and Greg smirked, he had been playing a game called chicken over the weekend. In this each player takes a lighted cigarette and stubs it out on his skin. The winner is the one who carries on longest, that is who bears the physical pain and inflicts the worst injuries, on this occasion Greg. (The use of the male gender here reflects the fact that the participants are almost always male, this being a macho game.)

Example: Carol came into a morning seminar thirty minutes late without giving either an apology or an excuse. She often appeared tired and dishevelled and on this occasion her noticeable fatigue was marked. During the seminar she started speaking on a couple of occasions and as the tutor could not make sense of what she was saying she asked her to repeat it. Carol responded by giggling in what seemed to be a very inappropriate manner. Afterwards the tutor asked Carol whether she would like to have a chat with her; Carol declined insisting she felt all right. A fortnight later the same tutor marked an essay which confirmed her suspicions that Carol was concentrating poorly, it was well below her usual standard. As she now had good reason to be concerned the tutor insisted on seeing Carol immediately after the next seminar.

Carol had a rather strange mixture of brightness and bleariness in her eyes, they were bloodshot but simultaneously cold and sparkling. She looked tired, and the tutor remarked on this. Carol responded with prickly anger, saying it was not her business to check on bedtimes, she was an adult and able to make that sort of decision herself. The tutor managed to steer sensitively around the subject and asked about Carol's leisure time. After a fairly difficult period during the early part of the meeting Carol began to open up more and described how she often went out with a group of friends, to all-night parties. To help them through the day it was the group culture to take stimulant drugs, or uppers as Carol called them. At first she was happy to spend her time like this but recently she had begun to worry about her work. Her friends appeared to have no such concerns and Carol continued to see them.

Greg and Carol had temporarily taken on the culture of their peer group as if it was an identity. They feared rejection from the group if they did not conform to expected behaviours. This thought was sufficiently devastating for them to indulge in self-damaging activities. In Greg's case this was overt and part of the macho image of his peer group. Carol's behaviour was more subtle, at least in the early days, but potentially just as destructive. They both occupied precarious positions within their peer groups.

As with all groups there is a strong possibility of expulsion if an individual takes a stand against the group. This risk is enhanced if the person making the challenge is not well established as a cult leader in the group, in which case they run a high risk of becoming an outsider, being ostracized in the process. Because of the heightened significance of peer groups to adolescents the lengths they will go to in order to stay an insider can be tremendous. Expulsion represents failure, rejection and loss of identity. It therefore takes a great deal of confidence and strength to break away and say no, that's not for me.

In these two examples the tutors had to make a decision about how far they should go in trying to engage with their students. This highlights one of the difficulties of the tutor role which at times can clash fruitlessly with adolescent developmental issues. Young people have a strong sense of omnipotence, or indestructibility, which results in their sometimes getting into dangerous situations. They are fragile but do not feel that way and because of this will tend to push at boundaries. The tutor needs to be aware of this in order to respond with sensitivity to the individual. There is a fine balance to be found between challenging risky behaviours versus encouraging the person to explore and by so doing allowing them to discover the limits of their safety. Too many rules and restrictions inhibit the capacity to learn and the excitement of discovery, too few can allow or covertly encourage the individual to take risks, some of which may end in disaster. Young people need to learn to take personal responsibility, but this is a gradual process which requires time and careful monitoring in order to develop to an optimal degree.

By their actions Greg and Carol brought attention to themselves. They both made visible statements which the tutor could not ignore, although initially Carol's tutor was prepared to let her late arrival ride. Greg had very deliberately rolled up his sleeves to show his peers and his tutor his scars. He behaved as if he was feeling macho but inside, as he later revealed in private, he felt he was being pushed around. In demonstrating his injured arms to the tutor he could be communicating a cry for help. The same applied to Carol. The pull to be in the group was matched by an internal awareness of its dangers, and for both it required an external voice to put this into words. In support of this Greg and Carol were visibly relieved when the tutor intervened. They were reassured that their misdemeanours had not gone unnoticed.

Identity formation

In the case of both Greg and Carol membership of a peer group initially helped them to feel affirmed as people who were important in the world. They took on the collective identity of the group and this gave them a sense of personal worth and confidence.

For many adolescents peer groups form a bridge between child and adult identities. As children our identity, or sense of who we are, is strongly influenced by our parents. As part of their development adolescents need to break away from this, at least for a time, in order to establish the beginnings of their adult identity formation. One aspect of this process is reflected in the self-questioning so common at this time of life. Part of adolescent development involves living through an existential crisis, the degree of severity of this varying greatly between individuals. Who am I? What is the purpose of life? Why are we here? These are a just a few of the questions deliberated on during this time.

An individual may be attracted to a group for a number of reasons but always there is some aspect of the group with which they strongly identify. The group contains a part of the individual's identity, something they can feel close to. In all social groupings this is the case, however in adolescence the group identity is often taken on in an extreme manner. For instance the wearing of similar clothes heightens an individual's sense of sharing an identity with another.

Adolescents often need to try out different aspects of their personality and tend to do this by attaching themselves sequentially to a number of different peer groups, each representing a particular function. They try on groups as we might try on clothes, to see how they fit. By doing this they get a sense of who they are, what their personality is, and over the course of time develop a central sense of self. Carol and Greg gradually came to realize that the peer groups they belonged to represented a destructive aspect of themselves and therefore were not, in the long term, healthy environments. They subsequently moved on to form relationships through which they were able to mature.

Regression

As development does not occur in a simple sequential direction, so it follows that in the adolescent maturation alternates with a process known as regression. At one moment an adolescent can be relatively adult, another time they can be childlike. This oscillation between the two states is the usual manner of progression through adolescence. We all have a tendency to respond to stress in different ways. Adolescents, and to some extent adults, tend to regress, or return to a childlike state, when stressed. Usually this regression is transient, occasionally it becomes more fixed.

> *Example:* Susan was an A grade student from a family who were otherwise not academic. She was confident, outgoing and had many friends at school. On arrival at university this changed dramatically. Susan felt anxious and began to have sleepless nights in which she had a recurrent dream of her parents dying. During the second weekend she left to visit her parents. She confided that she was miserable, that she did not feel she fitted in with the other students, and wanted to leave university and return home.

> *Example:* Marion wanted training to be a teacher but found the first year of her course difficult. She could cope with the academic work and in many respects was a model student. At the beginning of each term she experienced profound feelings of home sickness manifest as anxiety, nervousness and butterflies in her stomach. Gradually she found it increasingly hard to eat, began to vomit after taking food and lost weight.

Susan and Marion showed signs of regressing to childlike dependency. The task of coping in the adult world filled them with anxiety and in response they wanted to go back to their parental home and be looked after. This is not at all unusual. The transitions involved in leaving home are tremendous, there are huge steps to be taken and often no easy way of breaking them down into more manageable sizes. Susan's distress was immediate, through encouragement from her parents she went back to university and sought out her tutor. With support from him, especially his understanding comment that most of her peers felt this way from time to time, she rapidly found her feet and made friends. Further attention to the problems experienced by first year students has been outlined in Chapter 2.

Marion's situation was more complex and she sought help via her doctor. She had a disorder known as anorexia, a recurrence of an illness which first affected her at the age of fourteen. Fortunately she recognized the signs and with them her need for expert guidance. Marion's anorexia was a form of regression in which she reverted to the position of a child, unable to feed herself, whereas previously she had been functioning almost as an adult person.

In counselling Marion talked about how she had always been her mother's favourite child, the youngest of seven and the baby of the family. Before leaving home Marion had worked for a year in the same home for elderly people as her mother. Although she had secured a place in higher education she had deferred this because at the time she did not yet feel ready. During counselling an understanding of her symptoms emerged. At one level Marion's anorexia represented her wish to keep the status quo, with mother looking after and sheltering her from the world of grown ups. At another level Marion was protecting her mother from losing her, the youngest child and the only one still at home, and having to face the issues involved in this process. Marion's regression into illness therefore fulfilled a dual purpose, she needed looking after and mother also needed to look after her. Through counselling Marion managed to overcome her eating problem and face the rigours of separating from her mother, later beginning to form a new, adult relationship in its place.

Prolonged dependency in higher education

Through Marion's regression she became more dependent on her mother. One of the major tasks facing the adolescent is to overcome dependency on parents and mature into a responsible independent adult.

In some respects being in higher education slows down this process of maturation by encouraging a high level of dependency. A paradoxical situation arises where a person is legally able to vote, have sexual intercourse, drive a car, buy alcohol and cigarettes, watch adult only certified films, and enjoy all the other trappings of the adult world. Simultaneously they are forced into a prolonged period of financial reliance on their parents, which also carries a level of emotional dependency. This can produce conflict, resentment, anger, rebellion or an over-developed level of conformity, none of which aids the process of psychological development. These issues were central for Peter and Roger, described earlier in this chapter. Other problems are commonly presented to tutors.

> *Example:* Liz, a medical student, went to see her tutor. She had problems with her work. At home were a younger sister, with whom she shared a room, and her parents. Liz liked to study late at night as she concentrated well then. The only quiet place in the house was the bedroom, but she disturbed her sister if she worked there.

Liz depended on her parents for financial support and it was significantly cheaper for her to live with them. Unfortunately this also limited her studies and a circular situation was created. In order to be a student she required her parents' support. But this support, although willingly given, impeded her academic development.

Liz presents a typical problem to which, as in her case, there is often no easy solution. The financial constraints faced by her parents were real and although they were not insistent on her continuing to live at home they did not have the means to support her living in lodgings. After talking over the problem with her tutor Liz embarked upon negotiations with her parents. As a result they agreed to give her enough money to purchase an evening meal at the university three times a week. This allowed her to study there and also to socialize with other students. She explained that it was important to spend some of her student life living away from home and although her parents could not support her financially for the five years duration of the course, they managed to do this for the last two, giving her a gradual increase in freedom. This was not Liz's ideal solution, but close enough for her to bear with it and continue her studies.

Not all parents are as understanding as Liz's. There may be deep-seated reasons which make it difficult for parents to let go of their offspring. The example of Marion, the anorexic student described above, illustrates this. Marion's mother had brought up seven children; she had invested all her adult life to date in mothering. When the youngest child left home she was faced with a huge gap in her life, a situation often known as the 'empty nest syndrome'. In order to be successful Marion's progress towards independence had to be matched by a major adjustment in her mother. This was an overwhelming transition for both which resulted in retreat into illness and mutual dependency. Fortunately, Marion and her mother managed to work this through to a successful conclusion.

Sometimes parents refuse to provide financial support for their offspring. This can be based on cultural expectations, for instance that at the age of eighteen an individual should be earning their own income; on pride, hiding the fact that there is no money to pay out; or on other factors such as envy. Often parents see that their children have more opportunities than they did at an equivalent age. Many parents regard this as a good sign, however for some it may evoke powerful feelings of envy and deprivation. One way these can become manifest is through the withholding of financial support without which the student will find it very difficult, if not impossible, to proceed with their education.

> *Example:* Stan was an art student, a sensitive and anxious individual who would occasionally submit excellent pieces of creative work. Towards the end of his first year he requested to see his tutor to inform her he may not be returning in the autumn term. His father had refused to make his grant contribution and he was in serious financial difficulty. Father ran a family business and had always assumed Stan would follow in his footsteps. Stan thought differently, took up his place at college, and a rift ensued.

There was a significant emotional entanglement which was impeding Stan's creative potential. His tutor recognized the need for practical assistance and referred Stan to the Welfare Office where he was able to negotiate a substantial, low interest loan to see him through the next two years. Stan was also informed about the student counselling service and encouraged to attend to give him an opportunity to deal with some of the psychological issues which were brought to a head during this time.

Special problems of dependency occur in specific groups of students. These include postgraduates, who have an extended period of higher education, mature students, who often have families, and students from overseas. Because of the importance and complexity of the issues involved these groups of students will be considered in detail in Chapters 6 and 7.

Sexual development

Sexual maturation is an important part of adolescent development and an area which often poses difficulties which can spill over into the educational setting. Tutors may be approached by students with concerns or problems which they have found it impossible to talk about elsewhere. Because of this, and the difficulty most people experience in talking about sexual matters, it is important to approach the subject in a sensitive, empathic, and non-judgemental manner.

Confidentiality

An essential first consideration when a student brings a personal problem to their tutor is confidentiality. This is particularly relevant when addressing issues related to sexuality. This poses difficulties for some tutors who feel out of their depth and wish to consult with colleagues. To avoid breaking confidentiality we suggest that in the course of discussions personal material such as names, or other information which may lead to the identification of an individual, are omitted.

> *Example:* A student confided in her tutor that she was pregnant. She was in a state of extreme panic, desperate to get help but not sure how to go about this. She was Catholic and in normal circumstances would seek advice through the church, but on this occasion felt too frightened and guilty to turn there.

The tutor recognized the problems and the need for urgent counselling. He was new and not aware of the forms of help available locally so discussed the situation, in general terms, with one of his academic colleagues. He found out about the existence of the counselling service and contacted the counsellor to ask whether this was the sort of case they took on, and how to refer. In this particular academic setting the counselling service offered a self-referral facility and an appointment within a few days. The tutor relayed this information to the student who followed it up with a request to be seen. There had been no point at which the student's name or details had been divulged, her privacy was assured.

Most institutions of higher education have links with a health centre or family planning clinic and it is one of the early duties of tutors to acquaint themselves with services available locally. The resources which are usually available and methods of linking up with them are explored further in Chapter 8. Information is often provided in a student handbook, there may be an equivalent source directory for tutors. It is also helpful to discover whether these services produce information leaflets covering subjects including contraception, sexually transmissible diseases, pregnancy testing, sexual orientation, Aids and HIV testing, and other areas which are of concern to many students. If so, it is wise to acquire a few.

Contraception

As students mature sexually they may require advice about contraception. Usually they will approach a friend or perhaps a parent in the first instance, occasionally it is an issue which is brought to a tutor. With the advent of Aids there is an increased emphasis on public education about contraception and the spread of sexually transmissible diseases, however it is still very common for individuals to have misapprehensions and to be ill-informed. In the adolescent population this is compounded by a strong sense of omnipotence captured in the phrase 'it won't happen to me'. Sadly, this is not the case. Unwanted pregnancy rates continue to rise, and with them figures for terminations of pregnancy, particularly in the young age group. Clearly it does happen to them, often with serious consequences.

Aids and HIV

Aids is a lethal infectious disease transmitted in a few very specific ways. One of these is via unprotected sexual intercourse with an infected person, others are by contact with contaminated blood either by transfusion, sharing needles, or needlestick injury. These modes of transmission have in common the exchange of body fluids which contain the virus responsible for the disease known as Aids. A nightmare quality of this disease is that it is transmissible before it is clinically manifest, which means that the person carrying the virus may not be noticeably ill and may pass it on unwittingly. Many students, perhaps surprisingly, do not practice safe sex and therefore put themselves at risk. Here the role of the tutor is to help people make informed choices rather than shrug off the risks without full consideration. There may be occasions when a student is worried that they have contracted the virus and confides in the tutor. The tutor must respond to such a concern seriously and help the student to seek appropriate expert guidance.

Example: A dental student came to see her tutor in a state of panic. She had performed a minor dental procedure on a patient, under supervision, and had later found out that the patient was HIV positive. She was worried that she might have contracted the disease.

When the tutor, who was a dentist, explored the anxiety with this student she was able to reassure her that she was unlikely to have contracted the disease. There was no bleeding at the time of the treatment and the student had worn protective gloves. The risk of infection was minimal and the student was greatly reassured by this knowledge. She later went for HIV testing via her general practitioner and was found to be negative.

The anxieties of this student were paramount and to some extent fuelled by lack of knowledge. Because the tutor was well informed about Aids and its mode of transmission she was able to reduce the anxiety of the student considerably. The fact that the tutor was calm throughout the conversation served to reinforce this. In this instance there was only a relatively slight risk of infection, but the tutor may also come across situations where the risk is much higher.

Example: Carol, described earlier, was using drugs and for the most part smoking them or taking tablets. On one occasion she shared a needle with a group of regular drug users, putting herself at risk in doing so.

During the initial meeting with the tutor Carol acknowledged her fear that she might have contracted Aids. This fear had a secondary harmful effect in that once she became convinced she had a fatal illness she really felt that life was not worth living and increasingly turned to drugs in an attempt to blot out her feelings of depression and hopelessness. Thus a dangerous vicious cycle was established, her fears reinforcing the drug taking which in turn put her at increased risk. Carol eventually sought counselling to help her make an informed decision about whether to have an Aids test.

Sexual orientation

During sexual development many people are confronted with issues related to their sexual orientation.

Example: Pauline was having serious difficulty concentrating on her work. At the instigation of her tutor she sought help in the counselling service as she was preoccupied with a personal problem. At school she had a close relationship with a girl and noticed that she had strong sexual feelings towards her. Pauline told her friend about this, the friend responded that she was not lesbian and did not wish to engage in a sexual relationship with another girl. Although Pauline tried to keep the friendship going her friend backed off, presumably feeling threatened. Pauline was left confused and isolated, afraid to confide in anyone in case the same thing happened. She continued to be miserable through school and in her early months at college. Eventually it all became too much for her and at this point she had turned to her tutor feeling depressed and suicidal.

With the counsellor Pauline was able to talk openly about her sexual feelings without the risk of being judged or rejected. This was a tremendous relief and helped to lift the burden of guilt which had been weighing very heavily on her. As a result of this release of emotional pressure she found her concentration much improved. She continued to work on conflicts about her sexual orientation but this problem gained a different perspective in her life.

It is crucial that tutors respond in a non-judgemental manner to disclosures about sexual orientation, whatever their personal views may be. Being on the front line with students can at times be a daunting and demanding task and carries a responsibility which extends beyond the immediate role of tutorship. If Pauline's tutor had reacted with shock or horror to her disclosure, as the friend had done previously, it may have precipitated a severe withdrawal, depression, or even suicide. Such a response would have reinforced Pauline's feelings of guilt and isolation, making it very difficult for her to seek further help. Similarly, if the tutor had a *laissez-faire* attitude and responded 'well I don't see what the problem is' this could have been perceived as a rejection, the tutor not taking Pauline's worries seriously.

Sexual orientation is an issue for many adolescents. In traditional psychoanalytic circles a phase of homosexuality, whether or not overtly expressed, is viewed as part of the normal developmental process. The logical extension of this theory is that the continuance of homosexuality into adult life is evidence of arrested development. This theory was developed at a time when there were extremely strong taboos on homosexuality, reflected in laws prohibiting its practice between consenting males in the UK. There was no equivalent law for women, presumably because of denial of the occurrence of lesbianism.

Contemporary society is increasingly challenging the views that both homosexuality and lesbianism are abnormal or represent arrested development, yet prejudice continues to be widespread. This confusion is represented in the current law in the UK which prohibits sexual relationships between consenting males under the age of eighteen, despite the fact that the age of consent for heterosexuals is sixteen. This law may produce a dilemma for tutors: what should they do if faced with a disclosure by a male student who is under the age of twenty-one and participating in a homosexual relationship? In resolving this dilemma it is generally recognized that the tutor's first responsibility is to the student, therefore confidentiality must be maintained. The student's primary need is to have a secure, trusting relationship with a tutor who accepts them and who does not respond in a hostile manner. For the tutor it is correspondingly important that they are able to talk about such matters with a certain amount of ease, which may involve preparatory self-exploration about their views on homosexuality and lesbianism. We feel it is important to stress this point: these issues are emotive, as illustrated in the following vignette.

Example: Keith went to his male tutor in a state of extreme distress having been unable to sleep for three nights. He had facial bruises and was walking stiffly, holding himself rigid because he was in physical pain. His pain was also emotional. At the weekend he had attended a gay disco and on leaving was followed by a group of young men. They assaulted him, the attack clearly being motivated on grounds of Keith's sexual orientation. Keith was very frightened and shocked, although he had frequently experienced verbal abuse he had never previously been physically assaulted. After being seen in the local casualty department and treated for his injuries Keith recognized his need for psychological help and so approached his tutor.

Keith's tutor was shocked and horrified, although for different reasons. Keith's revelation about his sexuality came as a surprise. The tutor had no inkling that Keith was gay and was thrown into a state of panic, it had struck a raw nerve for him. In their meeting Keith picked this up and said 'You don't want to hear about this do you?' Fortunately the tutor had sufficient self-awareness and empathy with Keith to respond positively. He told Keith he was angry about what had happened to him and recognized his need for help. He arranged to see him again later in the week, promising to investigate available resources in the meantime. At their second meeting he gave Keith information about the counselling service, 'Gay Helpline', and a student support group for gay and lesbian people. Keith followed up these leads with beneficial effects.

Keith's tutor meantime sought help through the counselling service. This service was primarily orientated towards student problems but the counsellors also had a role in staff development and on this basis agreed to see him. Although the tutor was currently in a stable heterosexual relationship he had been involved in a number of brief homosexual encounters in the past. These had been secretive in nature, associated with a high level of guilt, and were brought to mind, with acutely uncomfortable consequences, by Keith's revelation. Through brief counselling he was able to come to terms with this in a way that freed him to deal with future student consultations.

Sexual abuse

Students may confide in their tutors that they have been, or are currently, in a sexually abusive relationship. In these instances specialist help, such as that provided by a counselling service, a general practitioner or another expert should be sought. There are several examples of this problem cited elsewhere, which illustrate some of the difficulties associated with sexual abuse, notably Helen in Chapter 5.

Rarely a student may confide that he or she is a perpetrator of sexual abuse. In the UK this is taken to mean that an adult is involved in a sexual relationship with an individual under the age of sixteen, and that this is against the wishes of the minor party. In such case the student's need for confidentiality is overridden by the law. If a tutor has either knowledge of, or strong grounds for suspicion that sexual abuse is occurring, professional advice should be sought with a view to instigating an investigation. If tutors fail to initiate action they may be guilty of collusion. In the first instance it would probably be wise to seek advice from a representative of the counselling service, a general practitioner, or social worker. In general it is not the duty of a tutor to act as an agent of law enforcement, however suspected sexual abuse is one instance where this course of action is appropriate. Here a young person is at risk and consequently protective action should be taken.

Summary

In this chapter we have given an overview of the problems of adolescence highlighting issues which interact with higher education. Particular emphasis has been placed on two areas: the development of adult identity, and sexuality, which are of central importance in adolescent development. In the exploration of specific examples attention has been given to the tutor's role and the conflict that it can present, specifically the need to present the student with a balance between care and control. This balance is not easy to find, it is perhaps impossible to get it right all the time. Getting it right at least some of the time is the first step. We hope consideration of these issues will help tutors approach their students with more understanding and that they will thereby be in a better position to provide or recommend appropriate sources of help.

5

Academic Difficulties and Study Skills

Almost all students worry about their capacity to learn at some stage of their educational career. It follows that this is probably the most frequent reason for a student to seek help from a tutor. In this chapter we will explore common problems which contribute to study difficulties and academic failure, describe how the tutor can recognize underlying causes, and suggest appropriate interventions.

As with all complaints experienced by students, study skills encompass a range of problems. At one end of the spectrum are students who are worried about their capacity to study effectively but who perform well in assignments, at the other extreme are students who have severe academic difficulties. Anxiety can be a major inhibition to learning and attention will be focused on recognizing this common problem. Once it is identified the tutor can help many over-anxious students to study more effectively by using a range of simple techniques to aid the development of study skills. Students with severe difficulties including those who are failing to fulfil course requirements may require specialist help. In these cases the task of the tutor is to identify this need and refer the student to the appropriate service or agency.

Anxiety

Anxiety is a normal, probably universal, human experience which occurs in response to threat. Threat can be evoked by an examination, essay, competition, oral presentation, a lecturer with a sharp tongue, entering the common room, buying a round of drinks, a social invitation, thunder, a spider, and so on – the list is long.

Anxiety is manifest in many guises. It is sometimes experienced as excessive worry where it is easy to identify. Another way anxiety can make itself felt is through bodily symptoms such as sweating, shaking, blushing, palpitations, breathlessness or pain. The following examples illustrate the variety of forms anxiety can take.

Example: Margaret found herself unable to sleep after working hard in the evenings. She would go to bed but her mind was still on her work, going over the same issue again and again. She worried about her exams, if she slept badly the night before she might fail because she was too tired to concentrate. The more she worried the more she lay awake, which served to reinforce her anxiety in a vicious cycle from which she could not break free.

Example: John went to his doctor with shoulder and neck pain. He had no underlying physical problems. The pain was due to muscle tension. He was not aware of anxiety affecting him but was so wound up he held himself rigid as he worked.

Example: Robert knocked on his tutor's door, he was pale and sweaty, unlike his usual self. He had a long-standing stammer, which he generally controlled well, but on this occasion it took him several minutes to say a few words. In the city centre he had been threatened at knife point and forced to hand over his wallet. He had been in a state of panic since the assault.

The role of the tutor

Each of the above examples illustrates a presentation of anxiety. In Margaret's case the anxiety was overt or, to put it another way, it was experienced directly, as psychic anxiety. The tutor suggested she reorganize her study habits and together they drew up a timetable in which she studied for two hours each evening then had a leisure period before retiring to bed. She would use this time to chat to flatmates, phone a friend, have a bath, visit the social club, take some exercise, or read a novel. This helped her to relax and took her mind off work, as a consequence her sleep improved. Simple interventions like this, an example of time management, can greatly improve concentration and efficiency and lead to a secondary lowering of anxiety. Further details of time management are given later in this chapter.

John's story is typical as it illustrates how anxiety can be converted into muscular tension in a process known as somatization. In this form it can be difficult to detect. Social stigmata tend to reinforce the process of denial which underlies physical presentations of anxiety. As a general rule male students find it especially difficult to openly acknowledge problems. Early socialization tends to discourage this as boy children are expected to be tough and resilient. By talking about worries they lay themselves open to accusations of being wimpish or sensitive and as a result may fear alienation from their peer group. John improved with a combination of time management, in which he was encouraged to break from his work for five minutes every half hour, and relaxation training, which helped him to identify muscular tension and learn strategies to reduce it. His confidence and sense of self-worth grew and in parallel his underlying anxiety lessened.

Robert experienced intense anxiety following a traumatic assault. Although physically unharmed he suffered a major psychological trauma; his very existence had been threatened. He was referred to the counselling service where, with the help of an experienced counsellor, he was given an opportunity to talk about his experiences and work through his anxiety. At one stage during this process he became extremely angry at his assailant, a not uncommon experience but one which can be self-damaging if it becomes fixated. Robert's tutor helped by being accessible, by listening, by giving him permission to acknowledge his need for help, and by pointing him in the right direction.

Phobias and panic attacks

Anxiety can be due to unpleasant past experiences in which the individual has become highly sensitized and develops panic symptoms which at first sight are out of proportion to the degree of threat of the provoking stimulus.

Example: Shaun was irritable in a biochemistry practical and took this out on George, his working partner and flatmate, until George eventually stormed out of the laboratory leaving a heavy atmosphere in his wake.

The tutor helped Shaun complete the experiment and in the course of this chatted to him. It turned out that there had been a disagreement on the way into the college. George had suggested taking a short cut and walking across a park. Shaun refused but did not explain why. The previous day as they walked past the park entrance he had seen a large dog running around, this reminded him of a time when he had been attacked and bitten by a dog. The thought of walking across the park and facing a dog, which to him represented a serious threat, threw Shaun into a state of panic, or abject terror. He was embarrassed about this and therefore chose not to confide in George, who experienced his panic as unreasonable irritability.

Example: Luke's tutor asked to see him because he repeatedly failed to attend small group seminars. Luke's written work was of excellent quality and he was clearly a conscientious student, the tutor was puzzled about his unexplained absence.

When he arrived for the appointment Luke appeared nervous and apprehensive. He had difficulty stringing his words together and the tutor listened patiently, struggling to make sense of what he was hearing. Gradually the pieces began to fit together. Luke had been anxious about speaking in front of people throughout his life. At sixth form college he was asked to present a short talk on a project. He was worried about this and consequently slept badly the preceding night. On the day his hands started shaking, he felt sweaty and nauseous, his tongue tied itself in knots and he was unable to speak. The experience was a nightmare made worse by the loss of face he subsequently faced with his peer group. When asked to present a short talk in the small group seminars he was reminded of this experience and thrown into a state of panic, the prospect scared him half to death.

Shaun and Luke experienced typical panic attacks. In Shaun's case this interfered with his friendship with George. After talking to his tutor he realized how his dog phobia was affecting him and decided to seek help. Both Shaun and Luke were referred to the counselling service. There they participated in an anxiety management course which taught active methods of relaxation followed by a specific treatment known as exposure therapy. In this the subject faces the feared situation in a series of graded exercises, a process called systematic desensitization in which fear is gradually defused (Wolpe, 1969).

As is often the case the anxiety experienced by these students was greatly reduced by their first act of talking about and acknowledging it. The tutors helped by listening in an understanding non-judgemental manner. If they had brushed aside their fears and acted as if there was nothing to be worried about it would have probably driven them to a deeper, more hidden level and rendered them less accessible to help.

Shaun made rapid progress and was soon able to walk around parks freely without fear. His relationship with George also improved. From the academic point of view Luke's problem was more disabling. He needed support from his tutor to start attending the seminars and initially was silent. Because the tutor understood his difficulty he was able to allow Luke to take a back seat for a time. As a consequence, he gradually became more active and his growing confidence eventually became apparent when he summoned up the courage to challenge some of the tutor's assertions!

Hidden anxiety

The above accounts of anxiety are fairly transparent. Most of us can relate to them and recognize some of our own experiences, albeit perhaps in a milder form. The hidden reasons for anxiety are accessible and easily brought into conscious awareness. This is not always the case. Sometimes it can be difficult to discern underlying causes, the roots of anxiety can be elusive.

Example: Helen was brought to the counselling service by her tutor after failing an examination. In the room she was unable to speak for the first ten minutes. She was extremely distressed, trembling, weeping and sat hunched in a chair, her head on her knees. Although the tutor had dealt with many distressed students she had not previously come across such a profound display of depression and distress and rightly sought expert guidance for her student.

Slowly over the course of weeks, as she developed a trusting relationship with the counsellor, Helen's story emerged. From the age of nine to eleven she had been sexually abused by her father who would sit her on his knee, unzip his trousers and tell Helen to touch his penis. She obeyed, and although frightened also obeyed his instruction to keep this a secret with him. Helen effectively buried the memory of this traumatic time until, at the age of twenty, two events occurred in rapid sequence. One evening she watched a documentary programme about sexual abuse on the television. A few days later she had a viva examination in which the examiner, an older man, instructed her to demonstrate a procedure while he watched. Helen found herself shaking uncontrollably as the memories of her experiences with her father swept back and overwhelmed her. She could not speak, became acutely distressed, and eventually her tutor was sent for.

With the help of the counsellor Helen explored the impact of her early experiences and after a period of time out returned to, and successfully completed, her studies. Helen's experiences of sexual abuse had been so traumatic her conscious mind could not bear them and the memories had been pushed away, deeply repressed in her unconscious. These memories had not completely disappeared though, and were brought back by the television documentary following which they hovered elusively at the edges of her conscious thought. Looking back she described a vague sense of knowing what had happened to her, coupled with disbelief, which made her think she was imagining things. Then in the viva examination an older man instructed Helen to perform a task while he observed and assessed her. This forcefully released the memories of abuse and with them a confusing mixture of feelings, anxiety, anger, guilt and depression being prominent.

Helen's anxiety represented a conflict, or dilemma. She loved her father and considered herself to be his favourite daughter, yet he had abused his power and position and in the process damaged her. The examiner symbolized her father, she wanted to please him by doing as he asked but felt a profound sense of danger which threatened to overwhelm her if she obeyed him. The conflict of action versus inaction created paralysis, and as a result Helen was frozen by fear. With the counsellor a further conflict was manifest, namely could she safely talk about her experiences? The counsellor was able to provide an environment where Helen could begin to develop trust and, in her own time, she confided in her. This allowed her to work through her conflicts and eventually return to her studies.

Summary on anxiety

Anxiety takes on many guises, it can be manifest in a direct or indirect psychic form, or be experienced as physical, or somatic, symptoms. When asked to describe how anxiety affects them a group of students produced the following list:

Restlessness, tension, irritability, fear, panic, lack of control, poor concentration, feelings of unreality, worry, preoccupation, need for reassurance, agitation, fidgeting, hyper-alertness, on edge, insomnia, indecisiveness, gloom, apprehension, avoidance, sweaty hands, palpitations, breathlessness, butterflies, tremor, frequent micturition, diarrhoea, nausea, vomiting, loss of appetite or comfort eating, nail biting, muscle tension, tendency to be tongue-tied or babble, increased or decreased sex drive, difficulty getting an erection, social withdrawal.

It can be seen that anxiety is a normal experience, given certain circumstances any one of us would feel anxious. The same students were asked to say what made them anxious:

Unfamiliar situations, new places, uncertainty, unpredictable outcome, previous unpleasant experiences, pressure to perform, decisions, examinations, interviews, competitive situations including sport, confrontation, public speaking, sex, spiders, poor opinion of self, low self-confidence.

Themes emerging include environmental stimuli such as competition, tests, challenge, change, and adverse past experiences. Internal factors are also important, notably self-worth and self-confidence. Internal factors mesh with external demands in adolescents where development puts the person into an arena of multiple changes and challenges, producing high levels of anxiety, as explored in Chapter 4. Some students commented that a little anxiety can improve performance, provided it can be kept under control.

Anxiety can be a major block to learning which students can be helped to overcome. Tutors, as mentioned earlier, are often the first port of call. It is therefore important that they can recognize anxiety, are able to assess when specialist help is needed, and have knowledge of how this might be provided locally. Simple counselling skills, active listening, empathizing, support, and gentle confrontation, as described in Chapter 3 are invaluable in aiding the identification of anxiety.

To help their work tutors should have a basic understanding of study skills and time management, which will be outlined in greater detail later in this chapter. They may also choose to find out more about anxiety management, relaxation and exposure techniques. Some of these can be done on a self-help basis using commercially available audio-tapes, however this is time-consuming and outside the scope of the role of the personal tutor. In severe cases which do not respond to these simple measures exploratory counselling, which aims to uncover and resolve underlying conflicts, is necessary. Here the student should most definitely be directed to a source of specialist help in order to minimize the risks and maximize the benefits of counselling.

Academic failure

Almost without exception courses in higher education are graded. A specific, measured, value is placed on a piece of work. It is judged by another person to be excellent, good, satisfactory, borderline, or unacceptable, a failure. However viewing this as purely an objective process does not take account of the student's personal response to being assigned a grade, or percentage.

> *Example:* Andrea burst into inconsolable weeping on finding she had B grades. She wanted to be the best, to be an A grade student, and anything less was perceived as abysmal failure. In sharp contrast Diane was delighted at getting a borderline pass grade, which to her represented a tremendous success.

Here both students sought help from their tutor because they were anxious about their impending examinations. Each of them thought they might fail, but their views of what constituted failure differed greatly. Success and failure are not simple objectively definable experiences, they are also highly subjective and complex personal responses. The prospect of failure commonly engenders anxiety, as described in the preceding section. In determining how to respond to this it is important to discriminate between actual and perceived failure and, when failure is actual, to try and find the underlying cause or causes.

Perceived failure

Students such as Andrea often set themselves very high standards which are difficult if not impossible to achieve. Beneath this wish to perform well there may be a deep sense of insecurity, low self-esteem and poor self-worth. This can be exaggerated by high expectations of others, notably parents. In this situation the student may feel forced into an extreme position and either push themselves to attain high grades, or conversely set course to fail in rebellious desperation.

Andrea came from a working-class background. Her mother had shown intellectual interest and promise while at school but had been pressurized by her family to leave at the first opportunity and obtain employment. She was determined Andrea should not suffer the same fate and encouraged her to pursue a degree course, which she did. In order to support Andrea through her education, her mother did overtime hours at work and was frequently exhausted. Andrea was well aware of the sacrifices and strain experienced by her mother and as a result drove herself harder and harder. She initially gained A grades but as she became more tense and anxious so her examination performance started to decline. This resulted in her feeling increasingly guilty and undeserving of her educational opportunity.

Andrea's tutor was able to reassure her that she was a bright and capable student who would easily pass the degree course. She was given advice about study skills, which helped her to be more economical with time, and encouraged to become involved in extra-curricular activities. As a result Andrea made a number of friends and developed more self-confidence. As a later spin-off the tutor was also able to give her information about the School of Continuing Studies which offered a wide range of courses for people wishing to return to academic study, just what her mother needed. Once her mother was putting energy into her own development Andrea was released from this pressure and its accompanying guilt.

Actual failure

Unfortunately many students who have academic difficulties are not noticed until they fail an examination or assignment.

Example: Kate's tutor asked to see her when she failed an essay assignment. She was pale and looked tired and told the tutor she had been ill with influenza for the past two weeks. She was not aware that with medical support she could have delayed the deadline for submission and instead struggled to hand it in on time.

Example: Trevor failed an examination. It subsequently came to light that his brother, a known haemophiliac, was found to be HIV positive the week prior to the examination.

Ideally tutors should encourage students to inform them of serious adverse life experiences which happen during their courses and may affect their capacity to study. Institutional policies vary but there is usually some flexibility in the system to accommodate transient difficulties including illness and acute crises, such as bad news or a bereavement. Delaying a deadline is one example. Often examiners will make an allowance in the form of a slight adjustment to marks obtained as in the case of Trevor, who usually performed consistently well.

When difficulties have been conveyed to the tutor it is essential that confidentiality is preserved when the student's problems are discussed. The degree of confidentiality should be negotiated and agreed with the student. Trevor's tutor informed the examination board that one of his close relatives had recently been diagnosed as having a probable terminal illness, which was sufficient information to relay and protected him from vulnerable and unnecessary exposure.

Academic failure can be a result of anxiety, as discussed earlier in this chapter. It is also more likely to occur when a student has psychological difficulties of one sort or another.

Example: Yasmin was called to see her tutor after failing an assignment. In the meeting she explained she was unhappy about studying law, this was the choice of her parents. Given a free rein she would have elected to pursue her interest in literature.

Example: Steve failed his first year biochemistry examinations, he wanted to study medicine but was not accepted onto the course.

Yasmin and Steve were both unhappy about the courses they were study-ing. This resulted in them being poorly motivated and they did not therefore do themselves justice in assessed work. Yasmin's tutor encouraged her to tell her parents how strongly she felt about her interest in literature and after initially fraught discussions they eventually agreed to her trans-ferring courses, this process being facilitated by her tutor. Steve required a period of counselling to come to terms with his experience of rejection. Later his initial reluctance was replaced by intense interest in the course.

At one level Yasmin and Steve were struggling with the development of their identities, as symbolized by their chosen courses of study. Other forms of identity struggle can inhibit the capacity to study.

Example: James found concentration difficult. He went to see his tutor to explain why his assignment was late. To his surprise the tutor was a ready listener and James quickly moved on from his prepared excuse to talk about his underlying concerns. He had recently split up from his girlfriend of two years, the couple were developing in differ-ent directions and gradually grew apart. Towards the end they decided to open their relationship and James had a brief sexual liaison with a man. Since then he had started to question his sexual orientation and with it his identity. This had become a major preoccupation which interfered with his concentration and capacity to work.

James's tutor empathized well, he could remember his own adolescent turmoil all too clearly. He saw James's struggle as a common adolescent problem and did not react with horror to his disclosure. He arranged a further meeting and in the intervening period phoned the counselling service. Without disclosing the student's identity he discussed his problems and how he might best help him. In the subsequent meeting James was much more relaxed. At the suggestion of the counsellor the tutor gave him information about the counselling service and after considering this James decided against a consultation. He felt relieved that he had got his problem off his chest and pleased that his tutor had accepted his difficulties without condemnation. He recognized the need to think about his sexuality but pre-ferred to do this himself, in his own time and space. His tutor acknowl-edged this choice and made it clear that James could see him again if he continued to experience difficulties.

Here the tutor helped James to contain his anxiety by being non-judgemental, empathic and supportive of his decisions. This had the effect of helping him to feel he was a valid person, irrespective of his sexual-ity. While continuing his psychological development James managed to get down to some effective academic work.

Psychological problems interfere with study. They can take the form of life events or developmental struggles. Physical problems can also cause difficulty, as in the case of Kate, where an acute illness made it impossible to study. Other physical factors can have an impact.

Example: Brian performed poorly in an examination. He failed to attend an appointment with his tutor and was brought along a few days later by a friend. His speech was slurred and he smelt of alcohol. The friend explained that his drinking had been a problem for some time, causing frequent arguments in the house they shared.

Example: Graham had difficulty concentrating in tutorials and his academic standard was low. At a meeting with his tutor he could hardly keep his eyes open, he was drowsy and uncommunicative. It turned out that he had a history of epilepsy and was taking regular medication. His doctor was asked to see him and found that he was over-medicated, which caused him to be drowsy and to have poor concentration. His medication was subsequently altered, he remained free of fits, was noticeably more alert and his work improved.

Brian and Graham were both taking drugs which acted to reduce mental activity. Brian had a high level of anxiety and was using alcohol as a form of self-medication to tranquillize himself. When offered help with his problem he refused and eventually was asked to leave the course because of repeated failures. Graham was embarrassed to seek help because he saw his epilepsy as a major handicap and attributed his academic failure to this rather than to the medication.

Other noxious substances including solvents, cannabis, amphetamines, heroin, and ecstasy can impair academic performance. It is useful if the tutors are aware of this as it increases their capacity to recognize problems and refer individual students for appropriate help where necessary.

Specific learning difficulties

Occasionally study problems are due to more specific learning difficulties and require expert help and guidance.

Example: Mohammed was an A grade student who failed his first examination at college. It turned out that he had always had difficulty reading and writing, although he was a talented physicist. After careful specialist assessment of his problem Mohammed was diagnosed as having dyslexia, a specific learning difficulty which affects the acquisition of reading and writing skills. Prior to entering higher education he had chosen mathematical subjects in examinations, here the dyslexia did not reveal itself and he performed well. As part of his degree course he was required to write essays and because of his difficulty failed a paper.

Once the problem was recognized it was possible to offer Mohammed help in the form of specialist input to improve his reading and writing skills. In addition the examination board, on the advice of the specialist, agreed to give him extra time for written work.

Study skills

This section aims to present the tutor with a broad overview of basic techniques to promote study skills. These are easily learned and applied and can result in a greatly increased efficiency. They are a useful adjunct to the personal tutor's work.

The first essential ingredient for successful studying is a place to work. Not all students have easy access to an environment which facilitates concentration and effective study. Without basic minimal requirements such as warmth, peace and quiet students are unlikely to give their best.

Example: Bruce lived alone in a bed-sit where a small electric fan heater was the sole source of warmth. Mould grew on the walls. There was no cleaning equipment and he developed a persistent cough because of the high levels of dust and spores in the atmosphere. When he tried to work he felt cold and uncomfortable and found himself unable to concentrate.

Example: Alice, a medical student, was working for her end of year examinations. She shared a house with four students, all on different courses. Problems surfaced when they started to celebrate, as their examinations finished a fortnight before hers. Alice found herself unable to get down to work, she was both envious of and distracted by her peers.

After hearing Bruce's story his tutor contacted the student accommodation service and paved the way towards his eventual rehousing. His landlord was struck off the college list of approved student residences. Bruce benefited greatly from the change, his academic work improved alongside the friendships he developed as a consequence of living in shared accommodation.

Not all students will need this degree of assistance, Bruce was a shy retiring lad who found it particularly difficult to assert his needs. This had contributed to his problem as he felt obliged to accept the first offer of accommodation he could find rather than looking for something more suitable.

Alice found her own solution. She talked to her flatmates and they agreed to keep the noise down after 10 pm to allow her to sleep. During the early evening Alice worked in the library where she was surrounded by other students sitting late examinations. The atmosphere there was more conducive to work and she also gained through not being alone in her frustrations.

Alice was sufficiently aware of her needs to tackle her flatmates. This is easier said than done for most students. It takes confidence, assertiveness, and determination to confront members of an adolescent peer group, as in doing so the risks of rejection and alienation loom large.

Distractions from study time can be welcome, students have to find their own way of responding to tempting social invitations or extra-curricular activities. Distractions can also be generated from within in the form of displacement activities. One manifestation of this is that formerly tedious household chores suddenly become attractive to the student who has an urgent assignment to complete. Because higher education has less inherent structure than further education some students do not find the transition easy. Individual help with the organization of time and structuring of academic work may be required.

> *Example:* Diane, introduced in a previous example as the student who was delighted to scrape through her examinations, had just cause to be proud. She was a perfectionist who set herself ridiculously high standards, this made it impossible for her to complete a piece of work to her own satisfaction. Rather lamely Diane handed an essay to the tutor, one month late. It turned out she had spent an excessive amount of time completing it, at the expense of two other assignments and examination preparation. She was in a fix and she knew it!

> As Diane's problem is typical and one experienced by many students we shall give a detailed description of the help she was given. These basic principles can be adopted by most students with study problems.

Time management

Through exploration Diane was encouraged to examine her usual working pattern and identify times during the day when her concentration was at a peak. We all have natural circadian rhythms, times when we are relatively alert or drowsy. Effective time management can help us make good use of both extremes, working concentratedly when we are alert and resting in between. Patterns are individualistic, therefore time management is a personal task.

Diane's concentration profile was fairly constant as follows:

Level of concentration	24-hour time period
Maximum	09–12
	19–21
Moderate	12–16
	21–22
Poor	16–19
	22–09

As can be seen Diane has a typical twenty-four hour cycle of arousal. She works most effectively in the morning and mid-evening, least well in the early evening and overnight. Her work can be tailored around these times by allocating tasks that require a high level of concentration to the times she works best, performing more routine tasks during moderate periods of concentration, and resting during the remainder of the day.

Setting priorities
To assist Diane's time management she was asked to generate detailed information about all her course assignments and examinations, due dates, and weightings. This helped her gain an overview of the entire course. From this she developed a list of priorities and a plan for the year, broken down into three terms.

Bite-sized chunks
A central hurdle for Diane to overcome was her feeling of helplessness when she faced the huge volume of course work required. She confided in her tutor that she had a strong impulse to crawl into a corner and hibernate, never again to emerge. She had little confidence in her ability and required help in structuring and organizing her studies. Using the list of priorities she took the top item then wrote down the tasks she would need to do to complete it. Once she had reduced the item to manageable, bite-sized chunks her anxiety was defused and she was able to begin work. As a result her confidence increased which served to further reinforce her motivation to study.

Timetabling
Some tasks require higher levels of concentration than others. Effective timetabling takes this into consideration and matches peak times to complex tasks such as writing, statistical analysis, and examination revision. During moderate periods of concentration Diane read papers, edited and proofread essays, chased references, and practised computing skills. Her times of poor concentration were spent giving herself treats. For Diane this meant eating a favourite food, drinking a glass of wine, socializing, playing squash or lounging in a hot bath.

It may come as a surprise to many tutors to realize that a high proportion of students take little or no leisure time, particularly during periods of stress. The tutor can help by encouraging regular relaxation, in effect sanctioning it, thus alleviating the guilt so often engendered. Margaret, described earlier, responded well to this approach.

Within this process of timetabling it is important to have a degree of flexibility. If it is impossible to concentrate on a task it is sometimes helpful to move on to a different area of work. It is also useful to bear in mind that most people can concentrate for limited periods of time and build in mini-breaks, as did John.

Routine

Once a routine is established it becomes easier for the student to start and stop work. This is important, many students fail because they simply cannot get going and, once they have, are too anxious to stop and rest. This is dangerous, in a short space of time the student can become exhausted then demoralized. A downward spiral is then established which is difficult to reverse.

Developing a routine is facilitated by identifying a place to study. Bruce and Alice initially struggled with this but eventually succeeded. A private desk helps. Alice worked best in an isolated corner of the library but this does not suit everyone, individuals should be encouraged to experiment and find a place which feels right.

Self-monitoring

Diane enjoyed scheduling her work and slowly began to catch up on outstanding assignments. This process was not without hiccups. She was a perfectionist by nature and over a few weeks this tendency increasingly crept into her work plan. She spent long periods of time working out priorities and developed a numerical system which she applied to her schedule. Gradually this became more refined and time-consuming until it occupied a generous proportion of her timetable. Eventually she was spending most of her time planning rather than studying, determined to get the plan just right. She had almost gone full circle and had turned this method of study into an avoidance technique. Fortunately Diane recognized what was happening and was able to regain a more profitable style of study. She then began to monitor the distribution of her work with more care and the planning reverted to being a means to an end rather than an end in itself. More importantly Diane began to recognize how she constantly sabotaged herself, turning newly acquired skills into a disadvantage. Increasingly she saw how she was working against herself, could identify when this was occurring and so begin to change.

Performance skills

A student recently went to his tutor to ask how he could get through his exams. There is a short answer to this: preparation. He was disappointed, he had been looking for an easy option.

Preparation consists of learning and rehearsal. The techniques of time management, prioritizing, identifying tasks, and self-monitoring outlined above provide the basis and can be tailored to suit the individual student. Preparation should also be guided by the method of assessment. Different emphases are required for multiple choice, short answer, essay and practical examinations.

Individual students are responsible for their performance in higher education. They are in the best position to identify their own strengths and limitations and should be encouraged to approach the task of studying with these in mind. Active practice geared towards assessment can reduce anxiety in the test situation. The student who has difficulty writing essays will benefit from a few trial runs before facing the pressure in an examination. The tutor can assist this process by encouraging the student to take responsibility for choosing a likely essay title, writing the essay under self-imposed examination conditions, and then critically appraising the resulting written work. The tutor may also find time to read the essay and give feedback about performance but it is advisable for students to attempt to gauge this themselves in the long term and thereby build into their study skills a means of self-appraisal.

Performance anxiety can be a problem for some students. It is important for the tutor to be aware that an optimum level of anxiety improves performance. This is the case in a broad range of stressful situations including interviews, competitive sporting events, and academic examinations. If anxiety is too low the individual sometimes underachieves.

Example: Sally was an extremely bright and able student who wanted to continue her undergraduate research and applied for a post in the same department. Prior to the interview a member of staff, acting unethically, told her the job was hers for the taking. Sally felt relaxed as the interview approached, and as a result did not prepare fully or get herself 'psyched up' on the day. At interview she performed poorly and the post was offered to another candidate. The feedback after her interview indicated that she lacked enthusiasm and seemed overly laid back.

The opposite extreme is more common in the student population. Many students become intensely anxious about examinations and consequently perform poorly, their thinking capacity being swamped by anxiety.

Example: Charlie was a keen, interested student who always handed in excellent written work. He failed the first year examinations and later, in a meeting with his tutor, described having a typical panic attack on the day.

The tutor helped him in several ways. He listened to Charlie as he described what had happened, then went on to enquire about his preparation for the examinations. He was able to help Charlie draw up a more effective study strategy and to put his academic performance into context: the world would not end if he failed to complete the course. For Charlie the recognition that life could go on even if he had occasional disappointments was important. He also found help in the form of anxiety management training. Charlie resat his examinations and went on to successfully complete his course.

Summary

In this chapter we have described numerous difficulties experienced by students which impair their academic performance. The role of anxiety has been explored in depth. Attention has also been given to other factors such as personal relationship difficulties, alcohol or drug abuse, and adolescent turmoil which can present as study difficulties. Some of these themes are elaborated in other chapters. In this chapter our aim was to provide the tutor with a framework for developing an understanding of study problems accompanied by a description of useful interventions.

We are aware that most academics are heavily pressurized in their work and will not have sufficient time to offer individual help to many students. Our hope is that they will become more able to recognize the problems experienced by students as a result of this overview and hence to refer them to appropriate helping agencies or self-help materials.

6

Mature and Postgraduate Students

Many postgraduate students are mature students. Therefore we have organized this chapter to discuss first issues pertaining to mature students in general and secondly to consider the needs and concerns of postgraduate students in particular. While school leavers at the age of eighteen or nineteen years have traditionally constituted the vast majority of full-time students in our colleges and universities, a growing number of mature students now enrol for full-time courses. This is occurring because of new initiatives including positive action to help mature students through Access courses (see below), an awareness of the necessity of retraining arising out of economic recession, and in response to expressed needs of women due to the influence of the women's movement, which encourages women to maximize their educational opportunities.

Mature students come from a variety of backgrounds and include people who have worked for a number of years, women who have previously been 'working in the home', former offenders who have discovered education through rehabilitation programmes and students from overseas. They have in common the fact they are all studying or training either to enhance their career potential, or for their own personal development, or both.

Routes to higher education

Access courses

There are now a range of Access courses for people who have not previously had academic education beyond the age of sixteen. These courses are sometimes based in universities, but are more commonly found in colleges of further or higher education. Full-time students on these courses may be eligible for a discretionary award, part-time students can usually keep their unemployment or supplementary benefit. Courses vary but generally give primary emphasis to study skills and subsequently cover a broad range of subjects thus enabling students to explore interests and to develop their strengths. Access courses are designed to prepare students for entry into higher education. Most institutions of higher education will accept a quota of such students who do not fulfil the traditional entry requirements.

The aim of Access courses is to prepare students for entrance to university. Courses are intensive with as much emphasis on study skills and confidence building as on academic subjects. The main advantage of Access courses is that they are specifically geared towards adult learners. In addition to assistance with study skills, encouragement and support are an essential aspect of the training programme.

Although students come from diverse backgrounds the fact that they face similar challenges results in their gaining considerable benefit from peer group support as they struggle with the problems of academic learning. This support is enhanced by the structure of the courses, which tend to be based on small group teaching seminars. The university may seem harsh and impersonal after the intimacy of an Access course. The transition to a university course, where the emphasis is primarily on academic work, can be difficult. Mature students are usually highly motivated but it is inevitable that many will have to work hard to keep up with their younger fellow students, who arrive at university straight from school and the rigours of Advanced (A) Level GCE examinations.

Example: Sally was a thirty-seven year-old student with two teenage children. She had completed an Access course then progressed to an English Literature degree. After six weeks on the course she contacted her personal tutor to say that she was leaving. She was continually in tears and said she felt completely out of place on the course. She thought the other students were all much brighter than herself. Her marriage had broken down during the summer prior to starting the degree course and she had taken out an injunction against her husband as he had threatened to kill her. Sally had worked for the previous ten years in a fish and chip shop and now wanted to return there. Although she had enjoyed the Access course that she had taken prior to her admission to university the degree was different. She felt a misfit among the other students and decided that it had been a mistake to come.

Her tutor was sympathetic and supportive, he gave her time to explore her feelings. Despite his help Sally eventually decided to leave.

Sally's life-style had changed dramatically during her educational development. As she fulfilled more of her potential her husband and friends became alienated from her. The students on the Access course had been very supportive but the transition to university was not successful. She was trying to cope with too many changes at once and was unable to deal with the additional pressures of studying. She felt vulnerable and isolated and missed the supportive environment of her previous college and peer group.

In Sally's case there was too much anxiety for the personal tutor to handle. Nevertheless it was important that she was able to discuss her concerns with a member of the academic staff and the door was left open for her future return to the course. In circumstances that are less extreme the care and interest of a personal tutor can tip the balance between a student who stays on a course despite transitional difficulties and one who gives up.

Credit accumulation and transfer

The need for a more highly qualified workforce in Britain and the expansion of student numbers in higher education has given impetus to greater flexibility in awarding professional qualifications. Schemes include the Credit Accumulation and Transfer Scheme (CATS), and Accreditation of Prior Learning (APL). They give credits for previous courses or training schemes that count towards a higher qualification. This is an attractive option for many mature students as it values their previous experience. The drawback is that although practical or professional experience is valuable and important it does not prepare the individual for academic work. Students who have chosen this route often need specialised help and support to make the necessary adjustments to their learning style.

> *Example:* Damon had been a nurse for many years and had achieved status and respect in his professional life. Through a credit accumulation scheme he gained a place on a masters degree course in Management. He had been seconded to the course by his employer and started it full of confidence and determination. At the end of the first term he was shocked and upset to discover that he had failed an assignment which he considered to be of high standard.

Damon's personal tutor quickly diagnosed the problem. Although he had glowing references from his employer about his abilities it did not follow that he had the kind of experience that would help him through academic hurdles. Damon had not previously written academic essays and needed considerable tutoring to enable him to plan and execute this task. His tutor referred him to the study skills support service for specific help and gave him additional individual tutorials to restore his self-confidence and motivation. Damon was angry that the system had not accepted and valued his contribution. His feelings had to be heard, acknowledged and understood before he could move on to develop new skills.

A break in education

Some mature students enter higher education on the merits of their Advanced level GCE passes, examinations that may have been taken many years before. For this group study skills and the organization of time are often major problems because they are out of practice. Other mature students have gained the entry qualifications required through evening classes. Their endeavours have involved many hours of private study often in addition to full-time paid employment or the demands of managing a home and family. This can be an excellent preparation for studying for a degree. A further group of people return to learning while in prison and take examinations that prepare them for higher education on release. Such students may be well motivated towards achievement through education but readjustment to a new life-style and to a student community presents its own problems.

Example: Edgar had had a difficult life. He had been repeatedly physically abused by his father and spent many of his teenage years in remand homes as a result of his own violent behaviour, which mirrored that of his father. As an adult he was unemployed and involved in petty crime. He had several spells in prison, and was drifting aimlessly through life until he found himself in an open prison with excellent educational facilities. He made a good relationship with one of the teachers and started to read avidly. He developed an interest in psychology and, with the support of the probation service, continued his pursuit of knowledge when he left prison. He gained two A Level passes at GCE and started a university degree course in psychology.

Edgar's personal tutor was aware of his background and was prepared to help him if necessary. Edgar had extremely negative role models as a child and rebelled angrily against them. However through his relationships with several professional authority figures he had gained confidence and started to develop his strengths. He was also dependent on them for support. This need was enhanced because he was no longer in touch with his family of origin or his previous peer group of recidivist inmates. His personal tutor became his role model and reference point during his university career and was the person to whom he turned when he encountered problems.

Example: Denise was forty-five years old and had recently been divorced. She had left school at fifteen and while bringing up her children worked as a clerk typist. In the five years prior to embarking on her degree course she has attended evening classes at her local further education college where she gained five GCSEs and two A level GCEs. She chose a university a considerable distance from her home town because she wanted some time away from the demands of her family. She had worked hard on her self-confidence over the past few years, and was shocked by her emotional response to starting her new life. She felt ill at ease, underconfident, isolated and disorientated.

Denise turned to her tutor for support and encouragement, which he was happy to offer. Over the course of time she became increasingly demanding of her tutor and would seek him out when she encountered even minor problems. He responded by being kind but firm in setting boundaries for their relationship and encouraged her to attend meetings of the Mature Students Society. There Denise found another mature student of a similar age to befriend and within a few weeks they decided to share a flat, to their mutual benefit.

Edgar was emotionally much younger than his thirty years would suggest. Behind his tough exterior lay a vulnerable and insecure man. His academic work was not a problem to him, his self-esteem and relationships with others were his sources of stress. He needed the support and understanding of his tutor to overcome these difficulties. The ability to study is certainly an advantage to the mature student, but it does not mean that life as a student is plain sailing.

Denise felt like a child starting school for the first time. She had a new school bag, lots of paper, files and writing instruments, but was as lost and alone as she had felt starting nursery school. Sensitivity to her distress was vital to her adjustment and helped her make the transition from loneliness to joining her peer group. She was then able to become part of the institution and felt she belonged as a student.

Both Edgar and Denise were experiencing a major transition in their lives. Despite being 'grown up' they needed considerable support while they adjusted and found new friends. Personal tutors can find themselves overwhelmed by the demands of students like Edgar and Denise and a compromise needs to be found that gives students a clear understanding of what can be expected from their tutors. For example, in dealing with a demanding student it is usually more helpful to arrange to meet for half an hour at regular intervals than to suggest 'dropping in at any time'.

Mid-life issues

Not all mature students can be described as being in mid life, some will be in their early twenties and others may be in their late fifties or sixties. However it may be helpful to give some thought to the life-cycle and particularly to the phase described as mid life, say late twenties to mid-forties, as it provides a frame of reference for understanding the problems and issues that mature students may present.

To put mid life in context we need to consider what has gone before. Birth, babyhood, childhood, and adolescence are periods of rapid growth, change and transformation. For most people successful negotiation of the adolescent life stage, which we discussed in Chapter 4, leads to the formation of a secure identity. This is taken to indicate an ability to form intimate relationships, a set of values and beliefs that provide structure for life, and a sense of occupational identity.

In their twenties people tend to be preoccupied with the tasks of finding a partner, marriage, and having children, in conjunction with developing their careers. Mature students returning to full-time education during this period can be seen as fulfilling the latter of these tasks, developing a career path.

Erikson was a psychosocial theorist who mapped human growth and developmental stages from birth to death. He defined mid life as being a period that is characterized by the conflicting demands of generativity and self-absorption (Erikson, 1980). Productive energy has previously been absorbed in establishing a family, a home, and a pattern of work. During mid life this process continues but the potential for creativity and self-fulfilment is reviewed. A similar view was proposed by the psychoanalyst, Jung, who described the phase of mid life as being one of re-evaluation and reconstruction, a period of asking searching questions in the quest of resolution and wisdom (Stephens, 1990).

From this and other work the concept of the 'mid life crisis' has evolved. The process of re-evaluation sometimes leads to a period of emotional turmoil. As an internal examination of beliefs, values and meaning occurs so the external manifestation of this, life-style and relationships, also takes place. A mismatch invites change which has to be accommodated. This often occurs gradually, but a crisis may be precipitated. Occasionally a crisis is delayed by constant denial or resistance to change leading to frustration, depression, or anxiety. This can also be manifest as a physical illness or emotional breakdown.

Many mature students have emotional issues which relate to the mid life experience. They choose to study as a result of a gradual process of change or as the result of a re-evaluation of their lives following a major upheaval. When there has been a recent crisis, such as the break up of a partnership, students may be bruised and insecure and in need of support and guidance to help them establish their renewed independence. If a crisis has not yet occurred then watch out for it, because a major step such as taking on a degree course and all that entails can precipitate one. This needs a little further explanation.

Groups, families, or couples seek to achieve an equilibrium both in practical and emotional terms. Let us consider a couple with a long established relationship. Their lives are usually arranged, with or without argument, so that their basic needs are met. In other words practical arrangements are made so that money is available, food is purchased and cooked, living accommodation is procured and maintained, clothes are washed, and some balance of domestic responsibilities is achieved. Similarly, but much less obviously, there is a balance in the relationship in terms of emotional needs and expression, and psychological fit. When one partner begins to change either in practical terms, by relinquishing responsibility for certain duties, or in psychological terms, by becoming more independent and self-confident, this will inevitably produce a degree of dissonance in the relationship. The dissonance may be resolved as the partners adjust to the changes, which is more likely to occur when they are both able to recognize and freely discuss their concerns, or it may precipitate a crisis.

In all families or couples, however balanced and supportive they are, a major change such as taking on a university or college course will disturb the equilibrium. This may be easily and rapidly resolved but for many it precipitates a period of discomfort and turmoil. This domestic turmoil adds to the stress students experience from other sources such as study, essays, peer group, exams, money, travel. Thus mature students, despite their relatively high levels of motivation, are often a vulnerable group.

Many of the problems that mature students experience arise from a combination of their circumstances and personal development as outlined above. These problems could be marital, career orientated, or due to bereavement, either related to an actual death or a lost opportunity such as the potential for having children. It is unwise to assume that older students are less likely to need support than the younger ones.

Crisis in relationships

Example: Fiona was a first year mature student who was married with three young children. She had attended a further education college while her children were small, using their creche facilities, and had acquired good A Level grades that gained her a place at university. She was an excellent student, highly praised for her academic work. Her tutor was shocked and upset when she announced at the end of the first year that she was going to drop out. She explained tearfully that she could no longer tolerate the tension at home, where her husband had become increasingly antagonistic towards her attending college. She reported that he felt threatened by her academic success, as he did not have an education himself. The tutor was very sensitive to her dilemma, and did not push her to stay, although he gave her every encouragement to do so. Ultimately, he left the door open for her to return if and when she could.

Fiona left the course and went home determined to make the marriage work, which was her main priority at the time because of her three children. However the following year she returned to complete the course following the eventual breakdown of the marriage.

This is a clear example of the disruption of equilibrium described above. Through education Fiona changed her value system and her aspirations also changed. She developed self-confidence in her abilities to succeed and set in motion practical changes to meet her revised needs. Her husband was threatened by these changes and unable to accommodate them emotionally. When she left the course she hoped she could turn the clock back and renounce her new insight and knowledge in order to save her marriage. However it proved to be impossible to undo the internal development that had taken place. She soon became frustrated and dissatisfied with her life, then left her husband. Had she stayed in the relationship she may have suffered the fate of many who try to maintain a precarious equilibrium at the expense of their personal development, namely illness or breakdown. Fiona encountered many practical difficulties when she returned to college but eventually resolved them and successfully completed her course.

Example: David had been employed by a charitable trust in another part of the country. He decided that his career prospects were limited and that he should pursue a higher degree in Business Administration. He had been living with a partner for ten years before he started a masters degree course at university but went home only for weekends and holidays during the course. In April he missed a week and on his return made an appointment to see his tutor. He was distraught because his girlfriend had met someone else and wanted to end their relationship. He had made many sacrifices to take the degree but felt that the loss of his relationship was too much. His temptation was to drop out of the course so that he could go home and find a way to mend the relationship.

This is another example of the problems that can occur as the result of a major life change. In this instance the tutor referred David to the university counselling service, who helped him to cope with his grief, to understand more deeply the nature of his relationship, and to complete the course. His relationship with his tutor was also important, as he provided the link between David and the university. Immediately following the break up of the relationship David's work fell behind. Because he was aware of the situation the tutor ensured that he was not penalized for the late submission of his assignments.

Career change

One of the features of mid life for some people is the recognition of being mid career. They stop and take stock of the fact that they have been on a particular career path for twenty years or more and are faced with the prospect of another twenty. A re-evaluation may result in a decision to retrain, something not taken lightly because of financial and social constraints. Some mature students have had successful careers in respected professions but decide that it is time for a change. Such students are committed to their newly chosen path, but may occasionally have 'cold feet' as they experience a sense of bereavement for all that they have left behind, compounded by uncertainty about the future.

Example: Arthur had been in the army for twenty years and had achieved the rank of Major. He had retired and was retraining through a university higher degree in Engineering. Arthur had been used to commanding dozens of men, and to being in control of both people and activities. Although he wanted the degree to make him more employable, he made himself very unpopular with his fellow students, with his constant tales beginning, 'When I was in the army . . . we did it like this'.

Arthur was very lucky that his personal tutor had slightly more patience with him than his fellow students! The tutor arranged regular tutorials for Arthur with the aim of trying to help him integrate into a civilian world.

The tutor recognized that Arthur was isolated from his peer group. This had negative implications for his study, particularly as they had to complete several group projects. Moreover his chances of gaining employment were likely to be restricted by his attitudes. A less patient tutor would have had little chance of success with this student, but with sustained gentle confrontation Arthur changed enough to help him through the course and into a job.

Bereavement

Mid life is the period during which parents are most likely to die. Some people take this in their stride, for others it can be a devastating experience.

> *Example:* George was forty-one years old, studying for a degree in Biological Science. He was an only child and had always lived with his widowed mother. She was very proud of him and was looking forward to his graduation. Just before his final examinations she died suddenly whilst out shopping. To say that he was devastated by this event is an understatement. He was beside himself with grief and feelings of loss. He was horrified at the prospect of facing life alone. He had never had another significant relationship. There was no possibility of him taking his final examinations, and he was given the option of being considered for an aegrotat degree or repeating the year, a decision which he was unable to make. After spending several sessions with him talking around the problem his tutor felt rather out of her depth. She recognized George's mental state was more serious than a normal bereavement reaction and wisely referred him to the counselling service.

In this example the bereavement George suffered was a particular shock because he was plunged into a developmental crisis that he had failed to negotiate successfully during adolescence. He had not worked through separation from his parent(s) or individuation, the development of his own identity as a person. It is not within the remit of a personal tutor to cope with such a serious bereavement reaction. The tutor may be able to help with a more normal and straightforward bereavement process by listening, showing concern, offering support and sometimes practical help, such as extending deadlines for assignments and informing other staff that the student had a bereavement. Bereavement would usually be reported as such and is seen as a legitimate factor to be presented to exam boards as mitigating evidence in the event of poor performance.

Fertility

A major feature of mid life for women in particular is the loss of fertility. Women who have already had children face the loss of these children as they grow up and leave home, the 'empty nest syndrome'. Women who have not yet had children may reconsider their decision. Either group may choose to try to have a baby during their last years of fertility, or may grieve for the children they have never had, or for lost opportunities. For most women this is a silent process that does not impinge on their work or studies. For some it can become a source of disturbance that is not easily resolved.

> *Example:* Katherine was a bright and able PhD student who had returned to postgraduate education after a career working in a laboratory for a pharmaceutical company. She was forty-two years old, and in the past had had several relationships but was not currently in a partnership. She made good progress with her research for a while but after a year or so her interest waned and she was regularly absent from the university. Her supervisor made an appointment to see her and was concerned to find her looking unkempt and depressed. Katherine had spent a lot of time alone at home feeling awful and found it difficult to communicate with him. He recognized that she needed help and encouraged her to see a counsellor. She agreed reluctantly and an appointment was made. In her exploration with the counsellor she was able to talk about her grief at not having had a child. Earlier in her life she had put her career first and had not been interested in having a family but now that it was almost too late it had assumed central importance.

Katherine's supervisor was an important catalyst in helping her towards the intervention that she needed to facilitate the resolution of her conflict. Had he been less sensitive to her change of behaviour and her depressed mood she may not have been able to come to terms with her problem and return to her research.

Issues between the personal tutor and mature students

Mature students are usually well motivated to learn and may set themselves high standards. They are frequently quite vocal in a group of mixed students and may be the most inquisitive. At the same time they may be at a disadvantage compared to younger students with respect to their adaptability, the speed with which they are able to work, and their retentive capacities. As previously discussed they often have additional external pressures.

Mature students have often made many sacrifices to embark on a college career and as a result have high expectations of their educational experience and make substantial demands of their personal tutor. The relationship between tutor and student is also different, more akin to a peer relationship. An older person may feel isolated in a group of young people and consequently seek the company and friendship of an academic member of staff.

Friendships between staff and mature students are not uncommon, and sometimes such relationships become more intimate. A code of practice on sexual harassment is unlikely to rule against sexual relationships between adults, be they staff or students, who choose to be together. However it is important that personal tutors keep in mind the special role that they have been assigned in relating to students and do not abuse the power inherent in their status.

On the other hand the personal tutor could be half the age of the student! Although a substantially younger member of the academic staff may be professionally respected, age may be a barrier to self-disclosure in personal tutorials. If this feels as though it could be a potential problem one solution is to verbalize it with the tutee, making a point of discussing the alternative support systems available in the organization.

Postgraduate research students

Postgraduate students are often mature students. Some become mature as they extend their studies over many years. There are many taught postgraduate courses, both full- and part-time, leading to professional qualifications and higher degrees. The previous section has covered many of the issues relevant to mature postgraduate students. This section will focus on the personal tutorial role with postgraduate research students.

Postgraduate research students may be engaged in their studies either full-time, or part-time while employed elsewhere, or while working as a research assistant in the same institution or department. Each may be subject to different pressures, to meet the tight deadline of a three year full-time contract, or to fit in study with a full-time job, while retaining some leisure time.

Postgraduate research students are unlikely to have a personal tutor as such but all will have a supervisor who should fulfil many of the roles and functions of a tutor, as well as having other responsibilities. The supervisor will be a member of the academic staff with specialist knowledge and experience in the area of research chosen by the student. This is the person with whom the student will be most closely associated throughout their course of study.

The pastoral role of the supervisor

Academics may have excellent research skills and be highly respected in their field of study. However there has often been little preparation for the role of supervisor which requires particular communication skills and personal qualities. The task of a supervisor is to facilitate the student's academic development through the research process. This involves questioning, reading, developing methodology and design, analysis and

Figure 6.1 Factors in the supervision process

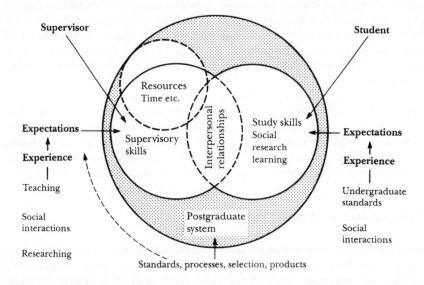

Source: Brown and Atkins (1990)

reflection and the ultimate presentation of a research project. The supervisor has a multifaceted role which incorporates technical knowledge and academic skill plus the capacity for personal and academic development.

In order to enhance an individual student's development the supervisor needs to identify their strengths and weaknesses, relevant experience, hopes and aspirations. Some supervisors claim to know their students when this knowledge is limited to an awareness of their subject interests and educational background. To really know a student requires a lot more. A postgraduate student's success or failure is a product of many factors including personal qualities, skills, abilities, motivation, financial security, personal circumstances, relationships, living accommodation and, last but not least, their relationship with their supervisor! The supervisor's relationship with their student needs to allow space for discussion of life issues that impact on the progress of academic work.

The supervisor is involved with all aspects of a student's project and is usually the only member of staff with whom the student has regular contact. A frequent complaint is that students do not see enough of their supervisors or that the supervisor's advice or guidance is too vague. There is little research knowledge about the supervision relationship but it has been found (Welsh, 1979) that both supervisor and research students see the relationship as having both a professional and a personal dimension. A good supervisor is one who shows both professional knowledge and expertise plus care and concern for the personal well-being of the student. It has been shown that students prefer their supervisors to work in a structured way and to show emotional warmth rather than to be emotionally cold and liberal, in the sense of not setting deadlines and boundaries (Brown and Atkins, 1990).

The roles and functions of a good supervisor are many and include the following:

1. Facilitator – enabling a process of thinking and developing thoughts and ideas.
2. Teacher – of study skills and research methods, as well as subject material.
3. Assessor – giving critical and constructive feedback and ultimately assessing the final project.
4. Counsellor – listening and giving support at times of difficulty.
5. Colleague – a person who shares similar interests with the student.
6. Manager – sets guidelines and deadlines, checks progress, but encourages personal responsibility and decision making.
7. Adviser – makes suggestions for managing the work, topics to consider, shares new ideas and concepts.

Common problems for research students

Rudd (1985) has researched the reasons for postgraduate failure and late completion of theses. He found that there was usually a combination of factors that contributed towards this problem, the most common being:

- poor project planning and management;
- methodological difficulties in the research;
- writing up;
- isolation;
- external personal problems;
- inadequate or negligent supervision.

In all these there is scope for supervisor intervention or support using the personal tutoring skills outlined elsewhere in this book. It is likely that supervisors will spend more time with their students than personal tutors and therefore be better acquainted with their personal and academic concerns.

Poor project planning and management

Supervisors cannot stand behind their students and watch every move but tightly structured supervision sessions, which help students focus on the task in hand and organize their work constructively from the beginning, are invaluable. An essential skill for research students is time management without which many projects are doomed to failure, however brilliant the student may be.

Time management has been discussed in some detail elsewhere in this text. People manage their time according to their temperament and previous experience. To some planning and scheduling, committing time, and sticking to timetables comes naturally. To others such activities go completely against their natural inclinations and self-discipline is gained only with great difficulty. Some students devote too little time to their studies whereas others work so hard they leave no space for leisure.

Workaholic students often go unrecognized until it is too late. They appear to be ideal students who submit assignments on schedule, are totally dedicated to their subject, and never mention personal issues. They are therefore assumed to be devoid of personal problems until there is a crisis. Leisure is an essential aspect of managing stress and students who work non-stop risk becoming overloaded.

> *Example:* Tony was a postgraduate doctoral student who made good progress with his PhD thesis until the deadline for submission approached, when he described himself as having a total mental block. He was suddenly unable to think, read, or write, and was beside himself with anxiety. His supervisor was shocked and amazed at this development as he saw Tony as a brilliant student who had always worked very hard and been successful. Tony now sought help and support with his 'mental block', which was a mystery to both of them. The supervisor felt deskilled in his relationship with Tony, which had previously been business-like and academic. The supervisor eventually referred Tony to the counselling service although unfortunately not until several months had elapsed, during which Tony sank deeper into despair.

In counselling it transpired that Tony had done nothing but work for the past four years. Apart from the occasional weekend visit to his mother he had not had a holiday during this time and had had little social contact with anyone. He had worked fourteen or fifteen hours a day, seven days a week in the department. His research had been the perfect cover for his fear of intimacy and personal relationships until he became so stressed and exhausted that this defence mechanism ceased to protect him.

He eventually obtained his PhD two years later when he had had psychotherapeutic help, time to recover from what was effectively a 'breakdown', and had re-ordered and balanced his life-style.

Tony's supervisor did not really know him at all. He related exclusively to the academic part of him and neglected his personal development. In effect he colluded with Tony over this and Tony felt that his work was the only part of himself over which he had control. On the surface Tony appeared to plan his work and organize the project perfectly. In effect his project management was a cover for a lack of self-management and both aspects need to be catered for.

Methodological difficulties in the research

> *Example:* Arnold was registered for a PhD in Biological Science. In consultation with his supervisor he chose a particular topic to study

and commenced his research. One aspect of this work was a replication of previous research. Arnold worked for two years on the project but the experiments in which he was engaged only worked spasmodically. His supervisor was unable to help him with the technical difficulties and it was eventually decided that Arnold should submit the work that had been completed for an MPhil rather than a PhD. Arnold was upset and frustrated by the decision and felt that he had wasted his time. He lost interest in the project and eventually found himself a job without completing a higher degree.

Arnold will have the sympathy of many who had embarked on a project which encounters methodological difficulties which appear to be insurmountable. Ideally students need to find topics for research that are manageable in the time available, of interest to the student, comprise original work, and are capable of a measurable outcome or solution. In this instance the task that Arnold embarked upon was too great for him to manage on his own. His supervisor had allowed him to be overly ambitious and had only limited knowledge with which to help and advise him.

An important aspect of the supervisor's work is knowing one's own limitations and ensuring these are covered elsewhere. For instance, a supervisor may recommend that the student consults other people for specific help with statistics.

Writing up
This topic has been covered in an earlier chapter on study skills. It is worth mentioning here as it is often an enormous problem for postgraduate students. There are many reasons why students find writing up projects difficult. Some find it hard to order their material and present their results coherently, others enjoy the research activity and find it hard to sit down and write. One student will procrastinate and leave the writing until tomorrow while another is a perfectionist who refuses to submit anything until it is absolutely perfect.

Example: Paul was a perfectionist. He pushed himself to the limit in every way and expected his best performance. He had always been highly stressed and the last months of writing up his PhD presented him with a challenge. His research was of an excellent standard and the write up had to do justice to it. He had a post-doctoral research job to go to when he finished but he could not finish the work. The deadline for completion approached and he became very distressed. His work was not quite right. He would have to write the last chapter again with only a week to go to submission. No amount of reassurance made any difference. He was advised to take a holiday, but he was too wound up to even think about it. Three months later, having missed the job, the thesis was finally submitted. He was disappointed and ashamed of it. The examiners thought it was brilliant.

There are a hundred and one variations on this theme. Writing up is a stressful task and a time when students need support and encouragement. Sometimes they also require a framework within which to work, for example weekly meetings with the supervisor to plan the next week's work and to check on progress. Writing up can start earlier than many students realize. Parts can be written up as papers or articles sometimes with the supervisor as joint author, although this can present problems.

Isolation

Students can become isolated for many reasons. They may come from overseas and find it difficult to integrate, they may work too hard and not give any space to socializing, or they may have a personal tendency towards being isolated, finding it hard to make contact with others. Supervisors may need to influence the system within which they work to help students overcome some of these problems, for example establishing research seminars in which students can bounce their thoughts and ideas off others, or making sure that there are adequate support systems for overseas students, as outlined elsewhere.

> *Example:* Susannah studied for her PhD for three years full-time and half-way through writing up she was offered and accepted a good job some distance from her university. She had been given another eighteen months to finish the research but, having not seen or heard of her for almost a year, her supervisor made contact. Susannah had made no progress with her writing up and had pushed the PhD to the back of her mind. She felt completely out of touch with the university and with the subject of her research now that she was pursuing new interests. She knew of no one locally with whom she could discuss the research work and felt distant from it. The supervisor arranged to visit her and they spent a day talking about her work and the writing up. The impetus was just what she needed to get going again and within three months the work was successfully submitted.

This is an example of one way in which students can become isolated as they reach the end of their project and illustrates how important it is for supervisors to stay in touch.

External personal problems

In this category the possibilities are infinite and many examples of personal problems which inhibit academic work are described elsewhere. Students do not live in a time capsule while they are studying and life goes on around them, bringing crises in both their external and internal worlds.

> *Example:* Julia was in the final stages of writing up her PhD thesis when her husband was killed in a car crash. Inevitably she was heartbroken and shocked by the incident and was unable to work for about six months. Throughout this period her supervisor kept in touch with her, at first offering sympathy and later support and the opportunity

to talk about her loss. Eventually Julia felt strong enough to recommence her work and rapidly completed it. She felt close to the supervisor and was very grateful for the support she had received. She also said that the continuous contact had been an important factor in helping her to come back.

This was a traumatic incident for all concerned, including the supervisor. We are not always well equipped to deal with bereavement but this particular supervisor handled it very well by not avoiding the emotion involved and keeping in touch. Julia responded by using this support and, when she was ready, by talking about her experiences of loss and grief. People often receive a lot of support in the days immediately following a bereavement but then are assumed to recover rapidly. If the supervisor had not stayed in touch with Julia it may have been much more painful to cross the bridge to return to her PhD.

Example: Pauline had spent a couple of years working in a hospital in a post that did not match her abilities after she completed her first degree and before enroling for a PhD. She had done well academically with her first degree but lacked any direction in career terms and drifted into a job which demanded very little from her. She was pleased to be back at the same university studying for her PhD and settled down to explore her academic interests. Five years later she had still not completed her PhD and showed little motivation to do so, although her work was of a good standard and the end was almost in sight. A final deadline to complete her work was set and she was thrown into a panic. Her supervisor had been oblivious to her personal world and, although she wondered why Pauline had taken so long over her work, it was not until she saw Pauline panic over the final deadline that she realized the problem went beyond laziness or lack of motivation. In a frank and open discussion one afternoon Pauline acknowledged that she was terrified of leaving the university and facing the world and the rest of her life.

Some students find great comfort and security in academic life, and find it difficult to leave. The transition to the world of employment can be too threatening, the implications of growing up and taking on responsibilities too great. Pauline was helped by professional counselling, her personal tutor/supervisor was the vital person who made help and change possible. It was her long-term relationship with Pauline and her in-depth knowledge and understanding of her that led to the recognition of a serious developmental problem. Once acknowledged the problem could be faced and eventually resolved.

Inadequate or negligent supervision
The common complaints that students have about their supervisors include the following: they have too few meetings, they appear disinterested, they

have little expertise in the subject area, they give no practical advice, they do not give direction, they fail to read work and give feedback within a reasonable time, they are absent too often, they lack research skills themselves, they are cold and distant.

Poor relationships with supervisors can produce disastrous results.

Example: Zoe was a twenty-eight year old electrical engineering PhD student. She referred herself to the counselling service because she was not making progress with her studies. She confided that she had a poor relationship with her supervisor, whom she considered to be sexist and unhelpful. He was the only member of the department who had the technical expertise to supervise her work. She complained that he was abroad for long periods of time and took her work with him. This resulted in excessive gaps between submitting scripts and receiving feedback on them. She claimed that he was inconsistent, changing his mind about what was right or wrong about her work. The worst thing was that she found him difficult to talk to. He did not listen when she tried to explain her ideas and snapped at her when she asked questions. She felt that he had no interest in her or her work and was consequently demoralized and miserable.

The counsellor recognized that the supervisory relationship was a real obstacle to Zoe's success and, having considered all the options, chose to give her regular personal support until the PhD was finished.

Zoe's problem is not unusual. Students often find that they have a personality clash with their supervisor or that the relationship is unhelpful and does not facilitate their learning. Sometimes the subject interest between supervisor and student is poorly matched, or the student does not feel supported or challenged by the supervisor.

Example: Gerry was interested in a specific aspect of theoretical physics. A supervisor was allocated to him and at first they related to each other quite well. However Gerry's work progressed very slowly which was partly because he was not good at organizing himself, compounded by the relaxed attitude of his supervisor who offered little guidance with either the subject or deadlines. Gerry often commented 'my supervisor's a nice guy but a hopeless supervisor'. Five years into a part-time PhD that supervisor left and Gerry was allocated another person who was much more directive and tough. Within fifteen months the PhD was completed.

Difficult students

We have made reference to the problems of poor supervision, so it is important to redress the balance by saying that there may also be problem students who do not respond to the help that supervisors are able to offer.

The 'know all'

Example: Terry registered for a PhD, saw his supervisor a couple of times then disappeared. His supervisor contacted him to arrange a further meeting but Terry did not turn up, neither did he send an apology. The supervisor contacted him again and Terry responded by saying that he did not need any help at the moment, he knew what he was doing. When Terry presented some work many months later the quality was poor and Terry was angry about the feedback he received. Despite this incident the same thing happened again six months later when the end of first year report was submitted. Terry was not accepted onto the next part of the programme and he dropped out.

Here the supervisor had attempted to guide Terry but he was unwilling to receive help. It may have been useful for the supervisor to have had a preliminary meeting with Terry to outline his expectations at the outset.

It's all their fault

Example: Jean attended her research supervision seminars and tutorials but never produced any work. She did not appear to be focusing on any specific area and her supervisor was concerned that she was wasting her time. Jean was full of excuses. Her flat was noisy, the books she wanted were never in the library, the word processors were always in use by others, her money had not come through, the registry had messed up her paperwork. After six months the final confrontation came, 'either produce some work or leave'. She left.

There are times when it is important to recognize that a student is struggling with the independent study required to successfully complete a further degree. This should be taken up with the student, giving an opportunity for any underlying problems to be explored. Once every avenue has been exhausted the supervisor has no choice but to acknowledge this with the student. It is kinder and more constructive for the student to help them withdraw with honour rather than struggle on for several years with little possibility of eventual success.

Summary

It would be convenient to think that mature and postgraduate students have sufficient resources to cope independently or with minimal pastoral care or assistance. As the examples in this chapter illustrate this does not always occur. Inevitably there will be many who succeed without a hitch, competing favourably with their younger colleagues in course work and examinations. However those that need support often need considerable input. The rewards of tutoring this group can be great. They are often highly motivated and respond positively to help which is offered.

We have elaborated on the role of supervisor in this chapter and drawn out some differences and similarities between this role and that of the personal tutor. Clearly there are many areas of overlap, supervisors have a specific responsibility for the academic progress of their students. The task of supervision incorporates many aspects of the role of the tutor and personal interest in students and their welfare is an essential aspect of the relationship.

7

Tutoring Students from Culturally Different Backgrounds

The student population of British institutions of higher education is multicultural. Britain is a mixed society and 'home' students come from a wide range of ethnic minority cultures, similarly students from many countries 'overseas' are increasingly encouraged to choose Britain for their studies. While it is important to treat all students as equals, and to give them the help and attention that they deserve, an awareness of and sensitivity to cultural differences is both necessary and rewarding, both in the classroom and when tutoring students.

'Home' students from ethnic minorities are likely to have been born in Britain, are used to the education system and do not need to adjust to life here. Nevertheless there may be times when their cultural expectations or religious beliefs demand informed understanding. 'Overseas' students require the same specialist understanding but in addition they have to adjust to a new life-style and education system.

Students who have a different cultural background from their tutors, the majority of whom are white British, experience all the problems commonly encountered by students. These have been described earlier and include difficulties with study skills, developmental issues, relationships or life crises. In addition they may have further difficulties arising from a cultural dimension. This should be taken into account by their tutors and teachers.

Inevitably we tend to judge people and situations according to our own life experiences, personal and cultural values. It is sometimes easy to come up with ideas and solutions that would fit our own framework. However to take account of another set of cultural norms and values requires the use of advanced empathic skills in order to understand a problem from the other person's perspective.

Example: Jinda was a bright, successful pharmacy student of South Asian origin who had lived all her life in Britain. She had enjoyed her university education but became depressed and withdrawn in her final year. She eventually confided to her tutor that she was anxious about going back to live in her parental home. She enjoyed the freedom of being away from home and had a white boyfriend. Now she was expected to return home and marry the man that her parents had chosen for her. She had met several possible suitors, her parents were flexible in allowing her to choose between them, but she felt controlled and constrained.

Example: Ali was an overseas student from Jordan. He was studying engineering and in most respects coped with the course very well. However he did not submit any assignments for his mathematics module, and did not attend either lectures or tutorials on the subject. At the end of the first year he failed the entire course because of his performance in mathematics. When his tutor, who was a man, discussed this with him Ali declared that he was not willing to have any work marked by a woman, as was the maths lecturer.

In both of these examples the tutor is faced with problems that are rooted in the cultural background of the students. A solution that would make sense in a white British culture is not tenable according to the student's cultural values.

Jinda's problem is difficult to handle but is one often encountered by personal tutors. Jinda is caught between two cultures and this produces internal conflicts for her. She has adopted the values and life-style of her peers while away at university but her parents hold their traditional cultural values. They expect her to conform to these and she knows that not to do so will bring shame on the family in the eyes of the community she comes from. This would be intolerable for her parents. She sees her choices as either to go along with the wishes and expectations of the family, or leave them altogether. Either option would cause extreme distress for the family and herself.

The personal tutor in whom Jinda confided was unable to provide an easy solution to her dilemma. The tutor's role in this instance would be to listen and communicate understanding of the predicament Jinda faces. Jinda will need to come to terms with whatever decision she makes about her future life-style. The tutor may be tempted to make a judgement about the behaviour of her parents or the decision that Jinda should make, either of which would be unhelpful. If Jinda became very distressed or depressed it would be appropriate to refer her to the counselling service for more in-depth help.

Ali had been brought up in a culture that does not allow women to hold positions of power or authority. For him to defer to the authority of a woman is a personal insult to him. His family had firmly reinforced this value system and he had been told that when he came to Britain he was not to allow himself to be degraded by women. The personal tutor again had a difficult task in helping Ali. It was not possible to change the lecturer for the maths course and academic standards would not allow Ali to pass the course without the maths module. Although the tutor may not agree with the values and expectations that Ali holds, it is essential that the tutor tries to understand Ali's point of view. Thereafter the tutor may be able to help Ali make some kind of bridge between his own culture and that of the society he has chosen for his higher education. Ali is unlikely to be able to survive three years of a degree course without encountering women in authority, as well as lecturers he will meet female housekeepers, wardens, police, doctors, and so on and he must make some adaptation to his current environment.

It would be easy to make judgements about Ali as being wrong, misguided or even sick, whereas Ali might make the same judgements about the host society or culture. Handled with sensitivity and understanding both parties may be able to learn something about cultural differences and cross cultural communication.

In these two examples the personal tutors involved have to be cautious in their response to the students and not be drawn into cultural stereotyping, making assumptions based on their experience of students of similar ethnic origin. Because one young girl of South Asian origin experiences conflict over an arranged marriage it does not follow that all such girls will experience similar problems. Families of South Asian ethnic origin in Britain vary in the extent to which they adhere to traditional cultural values.

Similarly, it would be wrong to assume that all Jordanians are likely to avoid women in authority. Cultural values are not fixed, they change over time and Jordanian cultural values are no exception. While it is useful to have knowledge about different cultures to aid awareness, it is imperative to avoid making stereotypical assumptions and to allow for diversity. Consider the British cultural caricature of someone with 'a stiff upper lip' who is cold, obsessed by the weather, eats fish and chips and watches cricket! Not many people fit this caricature.

It is difficult to convey an accurate message about cultural sensitivity, the only safe guideline that can be offered is to listen carefully to what is being said and to be alert for the cultural framework that influences attitudes and behaviour. Colour is not necessarily an indicator of cultural difference.

Example: Joe was a white American studying in Britain for a year on an exchange programme. He enjoyed his stay but found the university teaching programme very different from his experience in Florida. He had always done well 'back home' and was dismayed at the poor marks he received for his assignments. When it came to exam time he was in a panic because he had to write essays, all the examinations he had taken previously were made up of multiple choice questions. He expected to be encouraged for the work that he had produced and he felt put down by the lecturers.

Example: Sarah was a black student whose biological parents were of Nigerian origin. She had been adopted at birth by a white English middle class family living in Norwich. She had an East Anglian accent and had been brought up in the same way as her white adopted siblings. She had never been to Nigeria and said that she had been unaware of being black or 'different' until she was about nine years old. She was very irritated during her first weeks at university when people continually asked her where she came from and assumed that she was an overseas student new to Britain.

Joe was treated as though his background experience was similar to the home students although in many ways he felt quite alienated from the culture he found himself in. He looked similar, spoke the same language and assumptions were made from these superficial factors.

On the other hand, Sarah had the opposite reaction. Her experience, cultural and educational background were essentially British, but because her skin was black other assumptions were made about her which distressed her.

Overseas students

Universities and institutions of higher education recruit overseas students from all parts of the world. Some come to Britain with the help of scholarships from Government or British Council, others are supported by their families. Overseas students have high expectations of Britain and the British education system. For many their experience is a disappointment. Personal tutors have a crucial role with overseas students which can make the difference between a good or bad educational and emotional experience.

Selection and admission

Although the personal tutor may not be directly involved in admissions, subsequent involvement with their tutees may throw light on some of the issues which are vitally important in the recruitment of overseas students. They may wish to take these up with the university authorities to inform better practice.

> *Example:* Chong Ying arrived from Hong Kong to take a degree in mechanical engineering. On paper his qualifications were good and included a Cambridge First Certificate in English. It quickly became apparent that his ability to speak, read and write English was severely limited. Although he took extra classes in English, after the first two months of the course he was struggling both academically and emotionally. He could not understand lectures, was unable to complete assignments, and was lonely and isolated.

> *Example:* David came from Kenya to study medicine. His qualifications were excellent and his references very good. Initially he seemed to settle into the course well but after a few months became increasingly withdrawn. At the end of his second term he took a near fatal overdose

of tablets and was admitted to a psychiatric hospital suffering from clinical depression. It was later discovered that he had a long history of severe psychiatric problems in Kenya.

Both these students involved their personal tutors in many hours of work. Chong Ying looked to his personal tutor for help and support which was very difficult as communication was limited. David was a worry to many of the staff who alerted his personal tutor to his severe withdrawal. Following the overdose his tutor felt guilty because he had not done more to help.

In both cases the problems could have been avoided if the admissions procedure had been more thorough. Chong Ying could have been interviewed by the British Council in Hong Kong who would have recognized that his English was not of a sufficiently high standard. He could then have been channelled towards further English tuition prior to starting the course.

In David's case a full medical report would have revealed information about his psychiatric history. This does not necessarily mean that he would have been excluded from the course, but staff would have been alert to his problems. A supportive network could have been arranged involving his GP, a psychiatrist, and his personal tutor. It is possible that if this had occurred his breakdown could have been avoided.

In these cases the personal tutor had a lot of extra work for little reward in terms of the personal development of the students concerned. However, the time spent giving feedback and making recommendations to the admissions tutors was valuable and resulted in changes in admission policies occurring.

Induction

In Chapter 2 we highlighted some of the difficulties encountered by first year students. These are greatly magnified in overseas students who have to cope with major transitions. They often feel isolated living away from family and friends in an unfamiliar culture. A lot can be done to ease this process, to welcome them to Britain and to the university.

Example: Victoria was from Zimbabwe. She worked extremely hard to gain a scholarship to study dentistry in Britain. Her success was celebrated throughout her village and when she left home to come to Britain she was given a 'send off' party fit for a queen. She arrived full of pride, anxiety, excitement and expectations of her future home and course at university. She found her way to the university town with some difficulty and took a taxi to her hall of residence. She unpacked some of her things, washed and changed her clothes and went to her department to report her arrival. She encountered the departmental secretary who told her that enrolment was on Monday, to come back then. Victoria asked to see the head of department or his deputy, and was told that they were not available. She asked if she could have a book list so that she could purchase some books and was told that it would be given out on Monday. She had expected to be welcomed to Britain after all her efforts to get there and was bitterly disappointed that no one seemed to be interested in her arrival.

Victoria's story is not unusual. It is not told with the intention of provoking guilt or with the suggestion that red carpets should be laid out for overseas students, but to generate consideration of the impact of the first experiences of students from overseas. Induction programmes can facilitate a welcome for overseas students and convey the message that the institution cares.

There is a case for each university to employ a person with a specific brief to cover the welfare of overseas students. A specialist overseas student welfare officer can also take responsibility for coordinating an induction course, thus easing the burden on personal tutors whose valuable time can then be focused on getting to know the students personally rather than becoming caught up in too many practical matters. The overseas student welfare officer can also stimulate departmental efforts to welcome overseas students, including the development of a 'friendship' or 'buddy' system, whereby each overseas student is paired with a volunteer 'home student' who can help them to find their way around and make new friends.

Personal tutors often hold 'introduction sherry parties' which can be uncomfortable and cause high anxiety for some people, hence an unrelaxed atmosphere and stilted, self-conscious communication develops. A structured group session which gives a framework for introductions may be more productive, as described in Chapter 2. In addition a useful introductory exercise for a tutorial group with several overseas students is described here. All the students in the tutorial group are asked to write down five words which describe:

- their home town;
- their home country;
- their home;
- their expectations of university life.

Taking each topic in turn the students are asked to share their list with others and discuss some of the differences that emerge.

Later in the session the group of students are asked to write down five words to describe the town or the university that they are now in. They then go on to share and compare their first impressions. It may be interesting to hear the different impressions people get of the same place.

There are times when overseas students, or sometimes home students, arrive with special instructions from their parents. It is essential that personal tutors draw clear boundaries from the start about the limits of their role.

Example: A student handed the following letter to his tutor:

Dear Teacher, Please take good care of my son. He is a delicate child and needs a lot of care and attention. He needs to go to bed early, so that he can attend to his studies, and he must wash thoroughly each day. I think that he would benefit from some good friends, particularly a girl friend. I would be pleased if you could find him a nice young lady with whom he can walk around your beautiful gardens. Many thanks.

Clearly the personal tutor is not able to take on the role of chaperon, and would need to make that clear to the concerned parent. The tutor may also relay information about the help and support which is provided by the university, which includes regular contact with personal tutors but explaining the boundaries of that relationship.

Overseas student problems

Some problems that beset overseas students are inevitable. There is little or nothing that a personal tutor or institution can do to lessen the impact of, for example, the British climate, diet, language, or peculiarities of behaviour such as the propensity for queuing. Regrettably racial discrimination cannot be eliminated and may fuel a student's negative experience. Overseas students are likely to feel homesick and may have to work at developing friendships. They tend to gravitate towards students of their own nationality even though attempts are made at integration with British students. They may experience frustration if they cannot obtain their familiar traditional foods.

Some problems are avoidable or can be minimized if the institution takes the welfare of overseas students seriously. Provision can be made for married students both in terms of accommodation and support systems for non-student spouses. Financial arrangements should be made watertight before the student arrives. Similarly prior screening of academic and English ability can occur. Most importantly staff dealing with overseas students, particularly personal tutors, can be encouraged to develop sensitivity to their special needs and problems in order to minimize misunderstanding and ethnocentricity. However even given the very best of intentions and support systems, problems will occur.

Homesickness

Example: Raj was from the Indian subcontinent and had been seconded by his company to take a masters degree in Business Administration in Britain. He was married and arrived alone as his wife was six months pregnant and had opted to stay at home with his family. Although he was desperately lonely from day one he felt bound by duty to stay and complete the course. He sought the company of his personal tutor who was supportive and sympathetic but concerned about him. The baby was born six weeks prematurely and lived for only a few days. Raj was distraught and unable to concentrate on his work. His tutor noticed this and encouraged him to return to India to visit his wife. When he returned to Britain two weeks later Raj was

still upset by the unhappy experience, however he was able to settle
into his studies and adjust to life way from home.

Example: Maria was thirty-two years old and from Brazil. She too had
been sent to Britain by her employer to gain an EFL [English as a
Foreign Language] teacher's qualification. She found the course very
difficult and often despaired of ever completing it. All the students on
her course were from overseas but none were from Brazil. She was in
a flat with other students who were all aged eighteen and first year
undergraduates. Maria spent a great deal of money phoning her
family in Brazil because she felt lonely. Despite being a sociable, intelligent and attractive person she found it difficult to settle into university life. She liked her tutor, a woman of similar age, and a friendship
developed between them.

Homesickness is often a major concern for students from overseas. They
face many difficulties, including language and cultural barriers, in the
absence of their usual support network consisting of family and friends.
Self-confidence is enhanced by the affirmation and positive regard of people
around us. To be alone amongst strangers, with whom there is no historical
association, can be an alienating and negative experience which threatens
identity and self-esteem. This is to some extent inevitable although it
can be ameliorated by personal tutors taking a sympathetic interest in the
welfare of their overseas students. Raj and Maria relied heavily on the support of their tutors. They were both of a similar age to their tutors who
could identify with them. They benefited from the time that their
tutors spent befriending them and helping them to adapt to student life
in Britain.

Raj was in trouble before his tragedy occurred. The fact that he already
had a relationship with his tutor was of immense value when he received
the distressing news about the death of his child. He was able to trust her
judgement that two weeks away from his studies could easily be made up
later. Maria was lucky that she was able to form such a good relationship
with her tutor whose support was highly valued. As her tutor had to assess
Maria's work it was important to pay attention to the boundaries of their
relationship. When expectations are not clearly agreed between personal
tutors and students goodwill can develop into frustration and irritation to
the detriment of the tutoring relationship.

Some overseas students demand an excessive amount from their tutors,
as Raj had a tendency to do. When this occurs it is important to be aware
of all the support services available to help overseas students and to lobby
for their development, when they are inadequate or non-existent, through
appropriate university committees.

Secondment from employment
The fact that both Raj and Maria were seconded by their employer to study
in Britain was incidental to their main problem. For other students in those

circumstances the pressures arising from secondment can be so great as to be almost intolerable.

Example: Hussain was a forty-five year old married man with five children. At home in Kuwait he was a senior civil servant with the Ministry of Labour. There he was a respected member of the community and lived in a large house with servants. In Britain he was one of seventy students on a Public Sector Management course and lived in a small room in a hall of residence, while his wife and family remained in Kuwait. Hussain had all the problems of a mature student returning to academic work plus difficulties with language and domestic responsibilities. Further pressure was exerted because his government expected him to successfully complete the course then return to a promoted position. Despite working hard Hussain failed all his assignments and by the middle of the second term he was distraught. He confided in his tutor that he felt trapped and suicidal. He desperately wanted to leave the course and return to his family although in his mind this was a humiliating prospect. His personal tutor referred him to the student counselling service who together with the tutor co-ordinated a programme to enhance his study skills and organise his living arrangements.

Example: Leonard worked in a hospital in Tanzania and was sent to Britain to study personnel management. He was somewhat arrogant and had always been successful in both study and work. When Leonard started to get poor feedback for his assignments he was furious and at times became abusive to the lecturers concerned. The staff responded by becoming impatient with him and attention focused on his personal tutor to do something to help. A meeting with Leonard revealed that he was extremely anxious about failing the course, his employer was paying and this would make him seem foolish. Despite the support and understanding of the tutor Leonard continued to behave aggressively and demand a lot of attention. His marks did not improve and he started to miss deadlines for assignments. He then developed severe headaches and spent many hours under investigation at the medical centre. No cause could be found for his recurrent pain but Leonard now had a good reason for failing to submit assignments. At the end of the year Leonard returned home without his degree, having been too ill to complete it.

These examples portray the extent of the pressure overseas students may be under when their employer encourages and funds their study. In the examples given Hussain was eventually successful and Leonard, who suffered from headaches which may have been psychosomatic, was able to retire with honour. In both instances the personal tutors were heavily involved and coordinated their efforts with that of other agencies.

Family expectations

Overseas students, just like any other students, feel pressured by family expectations enhanced by the degree of financial support their parents give to send them to Britain.

> *Example:* Wong Lee was the eldest son of a large family in Malaysia. He came to Britain to study medicine and his family had made great sacrifices to find the money required. At the end of his course he was expected to return home to support the family. Wong was conscientious in the extreme and worked consistently hard for five years, having few friends and no interests outside his work. He caused no trouble and had little contact with his personal tutor. Everyone expected him to do well. When he had taken his final examination Wong sought out his personal tutor in despair.' He was convinced that he had failed, because he knew he had answered one question incorrectly. At first the tutor was incredulous that Wong could be so worried and proceeded to reassure him that he could not possibly have failed as he was an excellent student. His reassurance was to no avail and Wong continued to feel depressed and disturbed. The tutor then remembered his counselling skills and listened more carefully to what Wong was saying, reflecting his thoughts and his feelings. At this, the tension Wong had felt as a result of his obligations and his parents expectations during the previous five years began to surface.

In this example the student was ultimately successful in his studies but at great personal expense. Five years of his young life had been spent entirely devoted to his books and the strain that had put him under was considerable. It was fortunate in this instance that his tutor was able to help him work through his anxieties and frustrations and support him at a crucial time, because his view of the world had become so distorted that breakdown or suicide were possibilities. Some academics would see total devotion to study as a good thing, perhaps even the ideal way to spend time at university, with fun, relationships or other pastimes reserved for later. For most young people such dedication is not healthy and, unless some attention is paid to other personal needs, the result can be damaging in terms of readjustment to normal life.

Study difficulties

It is not unusual to find students studying subjects that are not of their choosing whether or not they are from overseas. Such a situation can lead to study difficulties which are discussed in detail in Chapter 5. However students from overseas add another dimension to the problems encountered. They are often working with a foreign language, difficult enough in itself, but may also have come from a country that has a broadly different education system.

> *Examples:* Ben was a Ghanaian student studying economics. He arrived with excellent references but failed several of his assignments in

the early part of the course. At first he received written feedback on his assignments, which he tried to acknowledge in order to do better in the next piece of work. When his marks did not improve he approached his personal tutor in distress. He had arrived in Britain confident of his abilities and he now felt deflated and anxious. The tutor asked Ben to bring an essay for her to read. She discovered that the content of Ben's essay was reasonable although the style in which he had written did not convey his ability to analyse and argue his points. Ben was surprised about this as his writing skills had not previously been questioned. The tutor referred him for some help from the study skills unit at the university and his work soon improved.

Example: Surinder was a travel and tourism management student from India who also arrived with excellent references. Her spoken English was very good, in contrast her written assignments received poor marks. She became depressed and despondent and consulted her tutor when she was on the point of leaving the course to return home. Her tutor discussed the comments which had been made about her work and looked at one of her assignments. At first sight the tutor was dismayed at the work because the problem seemed to reflect poor language skills. As he persevered with it he discovered that what she was trying to say was actually quite good but the presentation did not do it justice. Many people would have referred Surinder for English classes, however as her spoken English was so accurate this did not seem appropriate. He looked closely at her work and noticed that some of the words were jumbled with letters written backwards. He referred Surinder to the university health centre who arranged for her to be tested for dyslexia. The outcome was positive and she received the help that she needed to improve her performance.

In both of these cases less conscientious and observant personal tutors may have missed the problem altogether. The personal attention that these two students received, each involving about an hour of their tutor's time, paid dividends in terms of their education and well-being. Inevitably the first thought is about language difficulties but keeping in mind the fact that they have come from a different system, which does not necessarily have the same rules or expectations, is vital.

Religion
Religion is to many people an important aspect of life and overseas students are no exception. In Britain the occurrence of religious festivities have shaped the pattern of public holidays. There are few allowances made for religions which are not Christian yet are practised by many overseas students, which can lead to misunderstanding. For example Muslim students may wish to pray five times daily. Festivities for Jewish students such as Yom Kippur and Passover or Diwali for Hindu students are important events and allowances need to be made for their non-attendance on the relevant dates.

Students from some countries may have religious beliefs that are quite different from Christianity and the prevailing culture in Britain. It is important that tutors keep an open mind and broad perspective about this rather than jump to judgemental conclusions.

Example: Femi was a dental student from Botswana. During his first winter in Britain he slipped on some ice when walking to the university early one morning, fell awkwardly and broke his left leg. He was admitted to hospital for a few days and his personal tutor visited him. The tutor expressed his sympathy for Femi's accident and subsequent pain, adding that ice was a problem in winter. Femi replied that he was not at all sorry, in fact he was glad that something had happened. He had been expecting that something unpleasant would happen to him as he had disregarded his obligation to take on the role of head of his village to come to England, and the spirits do not forgive such acts easily. The personal tutor was at first surprised by this response, but later was able to think it through and put it into the context of Femi's background.

In Britain we tend to have an individualistic view of life, whereas there are other cultures that have a broader more familial or community perspective of collective responsibility. In the example given above Femi related not only to his family but also to his village, attributing considerable power to the community.

Financial problems

Many students have financial problems and they can be a major distraction from focusing on studying. When overseas students have such problems they can be severe and the cause of great distress.

Example: George was a Nigerian student whose father owned a thriving business in Lagos. He came to Britain to study with the full support of his family and expected to receive a monthly cheque to meet his needs. For the first year of his course all was well, however at the beginning of the second year the Nigerian Government tightened their exchange control regulations and George's money stopped arriving. His many telephone calls to his father assured him that everything possible was being done to despatch the money, but after several months nothing had arrived and George was becoming desperate. His personal tutor helped as much as possible, referring him to the university welfare fund for loans, but there was a limit to the funds available, consequently George endured great hardship. His studies suffered and his personal tutor was very concerned about him. Throughout the crisis the personal tutor arranged to see George each week for a progress report and review. Eventually the only option seemed to be that George withdraw temporarily from the course. He did so, then returned the following year. He was very grateful for the help, support and advice he had received from his tutor during a very difficult time and acknowledged just how awful those penniless few months had been.

Financial problems can trigger a moral dilemma for the tutors who are sometimes tempted to lend money to students. It is not advisable to do this, or only to do so in exceptional circumstances. However, it is essential that the college or university has a system for loaning money to students in an emergency as in George's case. The support that he received from the tutor was in itself highly valued by the student. It kept him going through an emotionally and physically distressing time.

Tutors can find themselves uncomfortably placed between the college authorities and their tutee over financial concerns.

Example: Sophia, from Turkey, was about to start the third year of her degree course when her father died at home in Istanbul. She went home for the funeral and missed the first two weeks of term. Her father's estate was put into the hands of a lawyer and when she returned to Britain she was unable to bring sufficient money to pay her fees. The university authorities declared that until the fees were paid, she was to be excluded from lectures. Her father's lawyer had told her to expect a delay of about three months before the money could be released.

Sophia was dealing with the grief of her father's sudden death together with the shock of being excluded from her studies at a crucial time. Her tutor was sympathetic and supportive. He was tempted to tell her to attend lectures anyway, but chose instead to put pressure on the authorities to allow her to do so. A letter was obtained from the lawyer, explaining the circumstances and promising that the money would be forthcoming. The tutor was very persistent to ensure that the attendance ban was speedily lifted.

In this instance the problem described might have been dealt with by the university welfare officer, overseas student officer, or even an advisory service of the student union. The ongoing support of the personal tutor would still have been valuable, so that the student was able to sustain a relationship with at least part of the organization although she felt hurt and rejected by another part.

War or civil unrest in the student's home country
Imagine being in another country for the purposes of study or even a holiday when something happens in your home country which makes it impossible or inadvisable to return there in the foreseeable future. Your family and friends are at home, communication systems have broken down and you have no idea whether they are dead or alive. This has been the fate of many overseas students studying in Britain in recent years. The change of regime in Iran, the Iran–Iraq war, the Tamil crisis in Sri Lanka, the Gulf War, and most recently wars resulting from the break up of Yugoslavia, have left many students stranded in Britain.

Example: Afiz was an Iraqi student studying for a postgraduate degree in computing. He had been living in England for many years and was looking forward to returning home at the end of his studies to serve his country. When Iraq invaded Kuwait he had just started the second year of the course. He had already suffered all the agonies of the Iran–Iraq war and had remained in Britain during this conflict at the insistence of his father who did not want Afiz to be drafted into the army. He was once again frightened for the safety of his family and the prospect of returning home seemed ever more distant. When the Gulf War started he was beside himself with anxiety not knowing how the British government would react to him and his fellow Iraqi students. He watched daily television reports of the destruction of his country. He was the victim of hate mail, presumably from fellow students, and felt isolated and perturbed. His personal tutor was able to empathize with his concerns and referred him to the counselling service.

Example: Marcovitch was a Bosnian student from Sarajevo. During the summer vacation of 1992 he did not return home to visit his family although he was worried sick for their safety. He watched daily reports of the destruction of Sarajevo on the television. He felt guilty for being safely out of the conflict while his family suffered. The British Council supported him financially and kept in regular touch to offer support and guidance. His personal tutor made a specific effort to contact him during the summer to lend her support. The personal tutor in this instance invited Marcovitch to her home each week. She felt powerless to help the people of Sarajevo and was pleased to be able to offer some comfort to her student.

The stress that overseas students face in these circumstances is extreme; their tenacity to survive and even study is remarkable. Support by personal tutors may seem insignificant in relation to their suffering, but is often vital in helping them survive the experience.

Disappointment

For many overseas students Britain is considered to be the promised land which offers endless opportunities. Their fantasies seldom correspond with reality. Many overseas students find Britain to be both physically and emotionally cold, expensive, and racist and they experience loneliness and disappointment. Students react in a variety of ways, some burying themselves in their work, others feeling let down, angry or depressed. Yet other students manifest their stress or distress in physical symptoms.

Example: Mary Loo was from Malaysia. Despite her expectations of student life in Britain she rapidly became disillusioned. She was placed in a flat with English students, with the aim of helping her to integrate, but she found her flatmates noisy, unfriendly and consumed by interests which she did not share. Within weeks Mary Loo was complaining of severe chest pains and her tutor advised her to visit the medical centre. There she was subjected to a variety of tests which threw no light on her symptoms. It was finally concluded by the doctors that her pains were stress related. That was both good news and bad news. The good news was that she was not suffering from a serious illness. The bad news was that she was still in pain and did not know how to deal with it. Her personal tutor was sympathetic and helpful and referred her to various support systems within the college, including the overseas students' club, and the befriending scheme. The latter was particularly useful as she made contact with another Malaysian girl who helped her to settle into her new life.

Meeting another Malaysian girl helped Mary Loo make a bridge between the two cultures. Overseas students often gain considerable comfort from developing friendships with their own national group. It is easy for 'home' students to be judgemental and comment that the overseas students stick together and do not attempt to make friends, but who can blame them when everything is so strange and they are far from home.

Cultural differences in the relationship with the personal tutor
There are many ways in which cultural differences are manifest in relationships and it is often important that personal tutors suspend their judgement until they have considered the cultural dimension of an encounter.

Example: Munikwa was a student from Zimbabwe. From a very early age he had been taught to respect people in authority, which meant agreeing with what they said because 'they knew best', looking at the floor when addressing them, and not asking questions. Munikwa had been well brought up and heeded his parents words, however this model of behaviour did not fit the requirements of a university undergraduate. He sat quietly in seminars and lectures, never asked for help when he did not understand, and made no approach to his personal tutor as he did not want to be any trouble.

Often personal tutors respect the autonomy of individuals and their right to pursue their studies without the help or involvement of their tutor. It can be difficult to approach students in a non-intrusive manner. Initially when Munikwa failed to attend personal tutorials his tutor made no effort to pursue this. Eventually his results revealed that Munikwa was not performing well and his tutor sought him out. Munikwa was shy and embarrassed and behaved as though he was about to be punished for his failure. Despite the tutor's persistent attempts to communicate her wish to help this attitude continued. The situation finally changed when the personal tutor invited Munikwa to talk about his background, his upbringing and his expectations of university life in Britain. She was then able to explore with him how education in Britain differed from his previous experience. She explained that he was expected to be more active and invited him to be more challenging and questioning, both verbally and in his written work. Although change did not come easily to this young man he became more able to engage with the tutor and attended their arranged meetings. His work subsequently improved.

> *Example:* Haziz was from the United Arab Emirates in his first year studying electronic engineering. He was angry when he received a low mark for his first assignment and protested to his personal tutor, insisting that the work deserved a higher mark and that it should be changed. The tutor found him offensive and aggressive and felt irritated with him, but despite this he dealt calmly with the situation and quietly asserted that the mark could not be changed. Eventually Haziz offered the tutor £50 to upgrade the result. Naturally his offer was refused, but the tutor became aware that although he seemed to be dealing with an aggressive and offensive student there was probably a cultural dimension to the encounter. The personal tutor then opened a discussion about how this matter would be handled in the student's home country. The student calmed down a little and explained that his father was so powerful in his town that the mark would probably be changed to avoid causing offence to him. The student gained some insight into his own behaviour and a valuable discussion about cultural differences ensued.

The personal tutors involved with these two examples had both attended a training course related to working with overseas students. They recognized the influence of a cultural dimension on the behaviour of the students and sought to unravel and clarify some of the underlying issues.

Munikwa had the potential to express himself with more confidence and Haziz was not aware of being rude in British terms. Both were behaving in the way they had been taught. Had the tutors taken the interaction at face value Munikwa would have been written off as shy and incompetent and Haziz as arrogant, aggressive, demanding and difficult, to be avoided at all costs. The sensitivity of the tutors facilitated increased self-awareness in the students and an improvement in their performance.

British students from ethnic minorities

The two largest ethnic minority groups in Britain are those of South Asian origin and of African-Caribbean origin. Students from ethnic minorities are under-represented in the student population, which can sometimes present a problem in itself. Similarly lecturers from an ethnic minority background are scarce, providing few role models. There are more students of South Asian than of African-Caribbean ethnic origin in higher education. Students of South Asian origin, particularly males, are encouraged to pursue traditional professional qualifications in medicine, dentistry, business studies and engineering. For these students the family has often been influential in the choice of subject, and the student is charged with studying for the benefit of the family as well as for themselves. This is often misunderstood by those unaware of cultural differences, particularly the tendency of some cultures to consider the needs of the group, family or community rather than of the individual, as tends to be encouraged in white British society.

Students of African-Caribbean origin usually find themselves in a small minority in universities. In a few cases the decision to pursue higher education may have been taken in the face of opposition from their family or community, to whom higher education may be regarded as 'selling out'. Higher education and certain professional occupations are sometimes considered to be elitist and racist, and to join them is tantamount to opting out of the struggle for equality and adopting the attitudes and values of the white majority.

Example: Rosanna was a student of African-Caribbean origin studying French. She existed on her student grant and a loan. She received no help from her parents, who disapproved of her decision to attend university. She was intelligent and capable, as well as being determined and hard working. Although she did not make many relationships with other students she developed a role with the student newspaper. She made little contact with her personal tutor other than attending the group sessions that were organized at the beginning of each term. At one of these meetings in her second year Rosanna was noticeably sullen and silent. Afterwards the tutor approached her and asked her how she was. Rosanna declared herself to be fine, and the tutor left it at that saying she was available at any time if Rosanna needed her. A few days later Rosanna knocked at her door, sat down and blurted out that she had decided to leave the course. The personal tutor listened carefully to her story, which revolved around Rosanna feeling isolated and unsupported. During the Easter holidays her family had, as always, taunted her saying she was stuck up, too good for them, too big for her boots, 'Miss smarty pants', traitor and so on. Returning to college and finding herself with no close friends or support there was just too much to bear, her resolve had broken. The personal tutor recognized that Rosanna's problems went deeper than she could handle and rightly referred her to the counselling service, while agreeing to continue to see her for ongoing support.

Example: Purdip, a twenty-seven year old man of south Asian origin, transferred to a pharmacy course having failed his final medical examinations at another university. He faced three more years of study to qualify in a profession that in his eyes was second best, in an attempt to redeem his failure. It soon became clear that he had difficulty with concentration, was poorly motivated and under achieved. His personal tutor confronted Purdip with his observations, telling him 'your heart did not seem to be in it'. Purdip was upset, acknowledged that he was disinterested, was fed up with studying and wished that he could leave, take a job of some sort, perhaps as a medical representative, and get on with his life. He considered this to be impossible as his parents would not allow it. Despite his discussions with the personal tutor Purdip felt there was no alternative but to continue. Within months he failed his end of term assessment and was asked to leave the course, thus the decision was taken out of his hands.

Example: Ashok was a young man of South Asian origin studying architecture. He confided in his personal tutor that he was unable to spend time studying because he was required to work until late at night in the family shop. His parents expected him to do well at university as well as taking responsibility for their business. Ashok found himself behind with his assignments and his parents accused him of wasting time during the day. The tutor offered to talk to Ashok's parents and explain the demands of the course, which Ashok declined. However he decided to have another attempt at talking to his parents himself armed with a copy of his timetable and the assignment schedule for the term. The personal tutor offered support which consisted of a rehearsal with Ashok presenting his case to the family.

These three examples illustrate the power that the family can have over decisions that individuals take. These students were caught between their family expectations and their own interests and desires. The personal tutor in each case responded with sensitivity to the cultural issues involved.

Racism

Many students of ethnic minority origins experience racism either overtly, in the form of a verbal or physical attack, or covertly, for example by being discriminated against when applying for a part in a play, a job, or standing for election to a student union position. Sometimes their experience has been so negative that they see all white people as racist and choose not to trust them.

Personal tutors need to become aware of their own values, prejudices and biases in order to work effectively with minority group students. They must inform themselves about cultural backgrounds and religions, while simultaneously avoiding stereotyping and typecasting. They need to feel comfortable with the difference between themselves and others, neither professing 'colour blindness', encompassed in the phrase 'we are all the same', nor ignoring differences in attitudes and beliefs. It is important to be able to accept and take seriously their students' experience of racism rather than trying to defend it or deny its existence.

Example: Parminder, a student of South Asian origin studying drama, was upset because she had not been given a part in a particular production. She complained to her tutor that the casting director, a fellow student, had discriminated against her because she was Asian. Although it was difficult to assess to what extent this was true, it was important that the personal tutor took her complaint seriously and gave her time to explore her anger and disappointment.

Example: Michael, a student of African-Caribbean origin, was in hospital after being attacked by a gang of white youths on his way home. He had been badly hurt, had his money stolen and was left bleeding on the pavement. He had been subjected to all kinds of insults, including being called, 'a dirty black bastard'. His personal tutor visited him in hospital and listened as Michael talked about his despair with the society that we lived in. The tutor felt ashamed to be white.

These examples illustrate both racism that is perceived and not proven and racism that is acted out in a vicious attack. It is perhaps easier to empathize with Michael, who suffered physically, than with Parminder, who was upset about the part she did not get. However both students warrant attention and understanding as they strive to cope with their distress. It is tempting, but would also be perceived as condescending, to reassure Parminder that the casting had been done fairly, or to tell Michael that he had been very unlucky and that the world was not as bad as he feared. In both cases patient listening and attempts at understanding these students' experiences as black people is more likely to be of benefit.

Summary

Students from ethnic minorities or from overseas can have all the problems of 'home' students with the added dimension of cultural difference and/or being thousands of miles away from their home. Overseas students deserve a little extra attention from their personal tutors, to assist them in making the cultural and personal adjustments to life in Britain. The more support systems the institutions have developed to help overseas students the less the burden will fall on personal tutors. It is therefore in their interests as well as the interests of individual students to lobby for adequate facilities to cope with their particular needs. The time and attention invested in overseas students is usually greatly appreciated and can make a profound difference to the overall experience of studying and living in Britain.

8

The Personal Tutor as Part of the Pastoral Care System

Personal tutors are an essential component of the pastoral care and support network of an institution of higher education. At times of crisis students turn in the first instance to the person with whom they feel most comfortable, who they think will listen to them without judgement. This is most likely to be a friend although when there are implications for academic work personal tutors may also be consulted. Personal tutors in turn need to be fully aware of the range of support services available in the institution so that appropriate referrals can be made.

In this chapter we give an overview of the range of support services that would be available in a typical university. Institutions of higher education vary in the provisions made for student support and in the way that services are organized and administered. Here we give an account of how various agencies function and pay specific attention to the way in which personal tutors can interact with each one. We include reference to a medical centre, Counselling Service, Student Advice Centre, careers service, accommodation service, chaplaincy, overseas student adviser, departmental support, physical recreation, student union support systems and finally a brief account of support services available in the wider community.

The medical centre

Many large universities have a medical centre attached to them, either functioning as an integral part of the institution or with a special arrangement for students and staff to be seen there. Within the medical centre there will usually be a number of doctors, often with a senior partner responsible for the overall practice, one or more secretaries, a receptionist, and a practice nurse.

In most large medical practices there is some degree of specialization within the group of doctors, thus one may have an interest in allergic disorders, another in psychological welfare, or women's health, and so on. The senior partner has overall responsibility for the administration of the practice and is influential in determining how it functions. This will include organization of the appointments system, arrangements for emergency cover and, in a university setting, liaison with the welfare and administrative structures within the institution.

Medical practitioners work with a code of conduct which is determined by their professional regulatory body, the General Medical Council. Aspects of medical practice essential to good patient care include confidentiality and the freedom to make clinical decisions which are in the patient's best interests. From the tutor's point of view it may be important to relay concern about a particular student to a doctor, but in return the tutor must accept that the doctor is bound to respect the patient's right to confidentiality. The doctor may be asked to submit a medical report in support of a student who is, or has been, unwell. In this situation the doctor will not usually give full details of the medical condition encountered, but will restrict the report to essential details, thus protecting the student's confidence.

> *Example:* Gavin consulted his doctor because he had a high temperature, felt exhausted and developed a skin rash. He was diagnosed as suffering from measles. Because of his illness he decided to return to his parental home and spent two weeks of the third term there. He was then late handing in an assignment, and asked the doctor to write to his tutor to explain that he had been ill. The doctor did so and reported that he had experienced a transient infectious disorder. Gavin in fact told his tutor that he had had measles, although the specific reason for his absence was not given in the medical report. Gavin was then allowed an extension of time to complete the outstanding piece of work.

There are circumstances when personal tutors may wish to refer a student to the medical centre, for instance if they feel a student needs medical treatment.

> *Example:* John consulted his tutor because he was feeling tired and lethargic. He said that he had been sleeping badly and was unable to concentrate on his work. The tutor asked John about his symptoms to ascertain whether they related to any emotional event or major change in his life, but John was unable to make any connections. She referred him to the doctor, partly because he may have required treatment, but also to ensure that a medical note was made of his condition in case his concentration did not improve and his academic performance suffered.

Thus links with a medical centre can usefully be made, and doctors' evidence can be used to support students who are ill. When determining which information to release doctors are principally concerned with the individual patient in treatment and work to protect their interests. This may be in contrast with the university which has to weigh up various aspects of a student's performance when determining which course of action to take.

Example: Declan had consistently failed to complete assignments on time and failed his first year exams. He sought medical help in the third term when he had influenza and his doctor wrote a report indicating that he had been ill and unable to work for two weeks. Because he had performed consistently poorly prior to his illness a decision was taken that he should re-sit the year.

There are instances when, for academic reasons, the doctor or nurses will encourage students to tell their personal tutor that they have a medical problem. They are not required to give specific details.

The counselling service

Most universities provide a counselling service for students and sometimes for staff. Provision varies in different institutions and, depending on resources available, including the counsellor/student ratio, a range of services will be provided. One model of a counselling service is restricted to seeing students referred by tutors or doctors, others give strict limits to the number of sessions an individual student can have, and other more generously resourced services give open access to staff and students. Some services provide only individual counselling, whereas others are able to offer groups and workshops to cover many of the issues that students regularly request help with, such as study skills, assertiveness, career development, or exam anxiety.

Professional counsellors come from diverse backgrounds including social work, clinical psychology, teaching, and nursing and have usually had several years of counselling training in addition to their original core training. Part of the counselling training usually involves personal exploration and development in order to enhance the counsellor's effectiveness.

There are many schools of counselling thought and practice. The major models of counselling are behavioural, person centred and psychodynamic, with many hybrid variations between them. These days many counsellors call themselves eclectic or integrative, as their training has covered aspects of some or each of the models. Behavioural, person centred and psychodynamic approaches to counselling are quite different. Behavioural counselling, or more often cognitive behavioural counselling, is derived from social learning theory and the counsellor has a role as educator. The symptoms presented by the client form the focus of the therapeutic work and attempts are made to understand and overcome them.

Person centred counselling is the major model of the existential or humanistic school of thought. Aspects of the relationship between the counsellor and the client form the central features of therapy. Carl Rogers (1951) extensively researched the counselling relationship. He concluded that the aspects of the counselling relationship required to facilitate the counselling process are empathy, unconditional acceptance, and genuineness. Empathy is conveyed by a moment to moment tracking of clients' feelings and personal experiences and an attempt by counsellors to put themselves in the clients' shoes. Counsellors give unconditional acceptance to their clients by showing respect and non-judgemental attitudes towards them. Genuineness requires counsellors to share their own thoughts and feelings with clients as they are appropriate. The relationship in this model is considered to be a real relationship between two human beings who strive to explore, understand, and re-evaluate experiences with the aim of seeing their concerns from a new, more enlightened perspective.

Psychodynamic counselling differs from behavioural counselling in that the focus of therapeutic work is on the underlying issues and conflicts that create symptoms rather than the symptoms themselves. It differs from the person centred approach in that the focal element is the transference relationship rather than the real relationship between counsellors and clients. The transference relationship describes distorted perceptions of counsellors which arise because of clients' previous relationships. For example, if a client has experienced authoritarian parenting which has resulted in their being passive and lacking assertiveness, they will relate to the counsellor as if they are authoritarian, and will expect to be told what to do. Another feature of the psychodynamic approach is the exploration of unconscious processes which affect conscious behaviour and experience.

To help us compare the three models of counselling let us explore how a person who experiences panic attacks would be understood and treated.

The behaviourist would see the panic attacks themselves as the problem and would focus on the management of anxiety leading up to and during an attack. This would include teaching relaxation techniques and the development of other coping strategies.

The person centred counsellor would seek to understand panic attacks in the context of the client's environment, relationships and understanding of themselves. The counsellor would help the client to discuss the problem, to feel accepted and understood and consequently to feel more confident in themselves to cope with situations and more able to trust their own intuition and judgement. They would also explore the personal meaning of the panic attack to the individual who experiences it.

The psychodynamic counsellor would understand panic attacks to be a symptom of unconscious conflict. The unconscious conflict can be described in terms of opposing emotional forces. Panic attacks may be a symptom of sexual conflict, where desire for sexual contact is encountered by an internal forbidding voice. The two conflicting messages create confusion and anxiety. Psychodynamic counsellors look for signs of unconscious conflict in their relationships with the clients. They offer interpretations which bring unconscious conflicts into conscious awareness where they can be understood and resolved.

An essential function of the counselling service is to make an assessment of students' needs when they present themselves for help. Part of the assessment is to determine the likely duration and focus of the counselling intervention. Some problems can be dealt with in one session whereas others require an extended period of time. The average number of sessions that student counselling services tend to report is between five and seven sessions. Counsellors should work within their limits and refer clients elsewhere when the need arises, for instance if they suspect there may be a psychiatric disorder or the client is suicidal the GP would be involved.

Group counselling
Some student problems can be more appropriately addressed in groups. Such groups might focus on social skills, study skills, assertiveness or interpersonal relationships. It is most appropriate to develop social skills in a group where interaction and feedback from peers is an integral part of the training programme. Students can learn a lot from each other in study skills groups through sharing their learning experiences.

Assertiveness training is a group activity which can benefit many young people as they learn through role play to face difficult situations with confidence.

Group psychotherapy has a lot to offer students who are motivated to change, particularly those whose difficulties are evident in their interpersonal relationships. The group is a closed, protected and confidential setting in which communication difficulties between members quickly become evident and thus can be explored and ultimately resolved with an experienced facilitator.

> *Example:* Simone referred herself to the counselling service because of her difficulty making friends. She felt lonely and rather isolated at university. In her assessment interview with the counsellor it transpired that she was an only child, she had grown up in a small village and although she had had a few friends at school, her social contact had been limited as they lived so far away from her. She had had a stable, happy childhood, had been successful in her studies but felt shy and lacking in confidence when it came to approaching other people.

The counsellor's opinion was that Simone's problems were interpersonal and it was decided that Simone could benefit from social skills training in a group. There she would be able to develop her interpersonal relating skills and improve her self-confidence alongside other students with similar problems. One of the advantages of group work is that students often make new friends, as did Simone.

> *Example:* Rex consulted the counsellor because he was having difficulty with his flatmates. They tended to be very noisy and throw parties that lasted into the night. He was feeling uncomfortable living there, he was unable to express his feelings and nervous that they would give him a hard time if he complained. In all other respects Rex seemed to be coping with his work and his life. The counsellor referred him to an assertiveness training group in order to help him to develop

specific skills which would allow more appropriate expression of his feelings and an increased sense of control over his environment.

Often the university has internal resources which can help individuals, but sometimes they will need a specialist support group or help that is based in the local community.

Example: Gary worked with the counsellor for eight sessions during which he explored his sexuality. He had always felt uncomfortable with his maleness, and during the counselling he acknowledged that he was a transsexual. The counselling helped him to accept this aspect of himself but he also needed the support of other people who shared his problem. The counsellor put him in touch with an organization called 'Friend', external to the university, that subsequently helped him to find a support group of transsexuals.

Example: Helena referred herself to the counsellor under pressure from her friends who were worried about her. She had lost a considerable amount of weight and her eating habits had become chaotic. She dieted for several days then would binge eat vast amounts of food, following which she vomited. The counsellor tried to work with her for a while but there was considerable resistance to change. Helena had become used to her symptoms and in a way enjoyed the attention that they afforded her. A support group for people suffering from bulimia (the medical term given to this condition) was set up by the local psychotherapy service and the counsellor suggested than Helena join it. Helena was reluctant at first, but did decide to join and found it very helpful.

The relationship between personal tutors and the counselling service
Personal tutors will have regular contact with the counselling service. Students may be able to refer themselves, in which case tutors may never know that their tutees have been counselled, but in some instances students will decide to tell their tutors that they are receiving help. Personal tutors are usually encouraged to ask for help and advice if they are concerned about a student they are seeing, while respecting confidentiality by ensuring the student is not identified.

It can be frustrating for a personal tutor if they refer a student to the counselling service and receive no feedback on their progress. The tutor may have had an initial consultation with the student during which they heard an outline of the problem, which has made them both curious and anxious to hear more. The tutor may want to know the 'diagnosis', to be informed about the 'treatment', or to know whether their 'hunch' is correct. The counsellor is bound by a professional code of ethics that inhibits them from giving feedback, even to the tutor who made the referral. Once the client steps over the threshold of the counsellor's room the process and content of the session becomes confidential to the participants, this confidentiality being broken only in exceptional circumstances when the student is a danger to himself or others.

Example: Sally visited the counselling service to discuss her distress at having been diagnosed as epileptic. She felt upset and ashamed of her problem and the social embarrassment it could cause. She had not told anyone in the university about her difficulties and was terrified that she would have a fit during lectures. The counsellor was able to help Sally come to terms with her diagnosis and then suggested she confide in her personal tutor so that appropriate support could be given by the department concerned.

Example: Joe talked to his personal tutor in the middle of his second year about a number of issues, including his thoughts of leaving college. The tutor tried to get to the bottom of the problem but Joe was rather vague and avoided the issue. The tutor then referred him to the counselling service, as he thought they might be able to help, before Joe made a final decision to leave. There Joe revealed his anxiety about making relationships with women. He did not leave college but instead worked through his concerns and successfully completed his degree. His tutor received no feedback from the counselling service other than a brief note to say thank you for the referral and that Joe had been seen. The tutor was curious about what had happened and a bit frustrated by being kept in the dark.

In the example of Sally the counsellor was the first person that she confided in but, having shared her concern once, she was able to speak to her tutor as well. This often happens. Once a problem has been aired and accepted it is easier to tell someone else.

The second example gives an insight into the importance of confidentiality within a counselling service. If the client had not been protected by confidentiality it is unlikely that he would have revealed his problem. The problem did not arise from his academic work or studies, although his work suffered considerably as a result of his anxiety. It would have been of no value to the tutor to know the content of the sessions other than to satisfy his curiosity. The tutor was acting professionally and correctly in referring the student for specialist help.

Counsellors are trained to facilitate self-awareness and personal insight that can lead to the resolution of personal difficulties. However their work can only be effective with a cooperative client who is motivated towards personal growth and change, and counselling is not a panacea for all ills.

It is sometimes tempting for tutors to refer or send their most difficult students to the counselling service in the hope of a miracle cure. The referral process requires skill and sensitivity. Unless students recognize that they have a problem, and wish to do something about it, the counselling service cannot help them.

Example: Alistair was a problem to the department and to his tutor. He attended lectures infrequently, missed assignment deadlines and regularly appeared to be under the influence of alcohol. His personal tutor confronted him with these problems, but Alistair shrugged them off. In desperation the tutor insisted that Alistair see the counsellor. An appointment was made which Alistair kept, arriving drunk and dishevelled. When asked why he had come he replied that he had been sent. When asked how he could be helped he responded that he did not want or need any help and promptly left.

This book contains many examples of students who have been helped by counselling. Alistair is not among this group. He was not sufficiently concerned about his behaviour to consider talking to another adult about it and did not wish to change either his behaviour or his attitude. In this example an alternative approach would have been for the tutor to make an appointment to see the counsellor and discuss his worries about Alistair. Alistair seems to make other people worry about him while he carries on in his own way. Tutors with students like Alistair need help to cope with their own anxiety, in order that they can put the responsibility back where it belongs. If Alistair does not conform to the requirements of the course, the tutor may have to consult with other staff to consider disciplinary action. This may be necessary if he continues to disrupt classes for other students or fails to hand in assignments. In other words the tutor may have to draw limits and make these explicit to the student.

Staff counselling
Many university counselling services in Britain make some provision for counselling staff. Some act purely as an information resource for staff and refer them on to local counselling services, some agree to see staff for a limited number of sessions, others have no limits on staff counselling. Personal tutors will certainly be encouraged to talk about their difficulties with students and can be reassured by the safety of the counselling environment when their own concerns emerge.

Example: Dr P made an appointment to see the counsellor concerning one of her students. In the meeting Dr P described how uncomfortable she felt with this student, he behaved in a superior way and would not listen to any help or advice. The student had just been offered a job in another university and was about to leave. He had been working on a project with Dr P and it seemed likely that he would leave with valuable data common to their research in his possession. Dr P had tried to discuss this with the student without success and was now feeling frustrated and angry. The counsellor was able to talk through the problem with Dr P who went on to tackle the student in a more rational and successful way.

University staff can have relationship difficulties just like any other human beings. When such problems occur they can be consuming both of time and emotional energy, leaving little space to meet students' needs. It is clearly an economical use of resources to help staff in need in order that they can function more effectively within the organization.

Example: When Dr A first consulted the counsellor he was contemplating suicide. After twenty-four years of marriage his wife had just left him for another man and his world seemed to have collapsed around him. He was angry and sad but felt that he was obliged to keep up appearances to the outside world that all was well. He had not told any of his colleagues about his wife's departure and was dreading the departmental dinner when he would have to make some excuse about her non-appearance. He felt ashamed to admit that his life was less than perfect and ending his life seemed like the only answer. The counsellor was able to help him cope with his grief and to restore his self-esteem. He confided in first one and then another of his colleagues who, contrary to his expectations, responded in a sympathetic and supportive manner.

The counselling service may also be the only place that staff can turn to in confidence when they experience problems with their teaching.

Example: Dr B had been an archaeologist until his department closed down. As a tenured lecturer he was offered the opportunity to retrain and chose to take a Masters degree in Information Technology. The course was one year full-time and, having successfully completed it, he returned to the university and was immediately given a full timetable teaching undergraduate computing and a module of a course similar to the one he had just completed. Within a month he was floundering and took a week off suffering from stress. On his return he made an appointment to see the counsellor to whom he poured out his despair. He had found the Masters degree course very challenging and felt that he had just scraped through it with considerable help from his fellow students and lecturers. He now felt a fraud in front of the students, being unable to answer many of their questions. He reported working very hard each evening to keep just one small step ahead of the students but realized that many of them, particularly the long-term computer enthusiasts, were way ahead of him.

The counsellor helped Dr B to detail a plan of action to change things. In the short term he decided to speak to the head of department and ask for some relief with his timetable, as well as asking a much more experienced lecturer in this area to be his mentor. New lecturers were automatically given this kind of support but the assumption had been made that as he had been teaching for twenty years he would not need it. He also decided to approach his ex-tutor for individual academic tutorials to help him get to grips with the areas that he was struggling with. The counsellor did not offer academic assistance but was able to help him put the problem into a perspective from which possible solutions could be explored.

The question is sometimes asked why universities need a counselling service. We would argue that a counselling service is an essential aspect of the support system available to staff and students alike to ensure that help is readily available, thereby enabling both to perform to the highest possible standard for the maximum amount of time. Many people do tackle problems without seeking professional help, but this is not always in their best interests. Although this volume focuses on universities we would suggest that many institutions could use a counselling service to good effect, from the perspective of improving morale and efficiency.

Student advice centre

Student advisory centres are to be found in most higher education institutions and are run by either the college and/or student unions. These services are known by a variety of titles including student welfare and student advice. They give advice to students on practical matters such as grants, supplementary benefit, tribunals and appeals as well as information about services available within and outside the college. Since student grants have been frozen these advice centres receive increasing requests for help with debt counselling and financial advice. They may also have access to hardship funds for students in an emergency. Students can approach the advice service themselves or be referred by a personal tutor or other. The advice centre may deal with complaints against college staff. When this occurs personal tutors may find themselves on either side of the table, defending a student or defending themselves.

Example: Rory was a gambling addict which had resulted in enormous debts and the closure by his bank of his current account. His problem had become a crisis for which he sought counselling but he also had an urgent practical problem for which he needed help. The debt counsellor who visited the advice centre once weekly helped him to assess his debts, consider ways of repaying them, and survive. She arranged for him to pay his grant cheque into a student union account, for his residence fees to be paid direct from the hardship fund, and for him to collect a small sum twice a week for his living expenses. Rory became quite depressed but the debt counsellor and the university counsellor were able to work together to support him through a very difficult time as he overcame his problems.

Example: Christine was a very attractive geology student in her third year. She asked for help and advice from the welfare service because she was feeling increasingly uncomfortable about her relationship with her personal tutor. He was a man in his forties who had helped her considerably during the second year of her course when her mother had died. However she reported that she was now feeling awkward with him because of the way he looked at her and various comments he had made about her appearance. The last time she had met with him he had placed himself between her and the door and moved towards her as if to embrace her. She had quickly pushed past him and left. She felt upset about this incident as in the past he had been very helpful but now she was reluctant to go near him. The student advisory officer was very supportive of Christine and explained the mechanism for making a formal complaint. In this instance the student decided to confront the tutor herself and clarify that she had no interest in him other than their professional relationship.

In this example Christine was able to tackle this difficult issue on her own and resolve the conflict, but some instances of sexual harassment are more extreme and cause severe distress. It is not unknown for lecturers or tutors to put pressure on a chosen student to provide them with sexual favours in return for good marks or help with assignments. Students can also be flirtatious and provocative, possibly unwittingly, and appear to invite more than professional contact. Sometimes the harassment is more complex when young students are at first flattered by the attention of a lecturer and feel privileged to be singled out for special attention but later feel hurt and confused if the relationship becomes an illicit affair. Such students will also have the right to complain about sexual harassment and the advice centre will be able to help them take appropriate action if they wish to lodge a formal complaint.

The student advice centre will also support students with their appeals against examination board decisions. They will usually help them to prepare their case and a representative will then accompany them to the appeal meeting.

Example: Alex failed the second year of his Fine Art and Painting degree course. He had worked very hard but felt that he had been penalized because his painting lecturer did not like his particular style of work. The advice centre helped him to prepare a case which included an independent assessment of some of his work undertaken by a lecturer from another university.

The student union welfare officer attended the appeal meeting with Alex and helped him to argue a coherent case. They were unable to change the original fail decision but Alex was granted permission to re-sit the second year.

The student advice centre has a wealth of information at its fingertips and busy personal tutors will benefit from being able to refer their tutees to the centre when the need arises.

Careers service
The careers service within an institution of higher education may fulfil a variety of functions. At best it will organize a careers fair, assist with job applications and interview skills. It will provide a library of career, vocational and educational information, careers fairs at which potential employers

meet prospective graduate employees, individual careers counselling and guidance, computerized vocational guidance systems, as well as facilitating career related seminars in departments. At worst it will have an employee or volunteer interested in career related issues who maintains a resource library. Clearly a more effective service is preferable, but whatever level of support the careers service provides it is a valuable asset for the personal tutor to which students with career related problems can be referred.

> *Example:* Tony was a management student who had to have a placement during his third year with a company. He had been for more than a dozen interviews and had been rejected as many times before consulting his tutor to discuss the problem. Tony had an unfortunate style of communication and it was not too difficult for his tutor to see why he had been rejected so many times. The tutor contacted the careers service who were running interview skills classes that term and referred Tony to the service. Tony also attended a class for students with specific difficulties related to their lack of social skills. As a result of this intervention both his social skills and interview skills improved and he was able to find and successfully complete a placement.

> *Example:* Janet had chosen to study English, which was her best A Level subject, at university. By the end of the first year she was beginning to think seriously about her career and, having dismissed journalism, librarianship, and teaching, she was worried about the future direction she would take. She made an appointment to see the careers officer who suggested that she use the computer software designed to help students think about their aptitudes and interests. The results of the occupational interest test and the subsequent interview with the careers officer prompted Janet to decide to change course and study psychology.

Personal tutors might not automatically think of the facilities of the careers service when faced with students who wish to change their courses, although careers officers are often well equipped to help such students by providing unbiased information.

Accommodation

Most universities have an accommodation service that either provides residences for students, or keeps records of accommodation available in the community, or both. It is important that personal tutors develop links with accommodation officers because there will be regular instances when students need help.

> *Example:* Charlotte was living in private accommodation about five miles from the university with a group of friends. She was quite happy

and settled there until she was attacked and sexually assaulted one evening on her way home from college. She was absent for a week and when she returned confided in her tutor. Charlotte was uncomfortable talking about her experience and reluctant to seek help elsewhere. She eventually agreed to see the counsellor and her tutor agreed to talk to the accommodation officer on her behalf about a residence place on campus, which was quickly arranged.

Residences staff

Most universities have their own halls of residence which have staff with a broad range of duties, some of whom will have a pastoral role including housekeepers, postgraduate student/tutors and wardens. Such staff can be valuable allies in working with students with troubles.

> *Example:* Sean's parents were killed in a road traffic accident. The news was broken to Sean at the university by the police on the afternoon of the incident in the presence of his personal tutor. The tutor used all his skills and humanity to comfort Sean and made arrangements for him to go and stay with his sister. When Sean came back after the funeral a week later he was clearly very subdued and depressed. His tutor worked with the housekeeper at Sean's hall of residence, the chaplain, and his flatmates, to ensure that he had a network of support to help him through the painful months ahead.

In many instances it is the housekeeper, warden or flatmate who first becomes aware of a problem. The housekeeper may notice that a student never goes to lectures, or a flatmate may confide in a warden their concern for a friend who is behaving in a strange manner.

> *Example:* Theresa was a third year student living in campus residences. Students in the block were required to vacate their rooms by 9.00 am on Thursdays so that they could be cleaned. One Thursday morning Mrs Adams, the cleaner, arrived as usual and started working on the rooms. When she opened Theresa's door she found her lying unconscious on the bed. She saw an empty bottle of tablets on the floor and immediately called for help. Theresa was taken to hospital, had her stomach washed out and survived. Theresa had often laughed and joked with the cleaning lady and may have chosen to take the tablets that morning because she knew she would be found. After the event, although Theresa was ashamed of her action, a supportive relationship developed between her and Mrs Adams and they often sat down to chat when she was around. Theresa had had a bad relationship with her own mother and found Mrs Adams warm and easy to confide in.

The case described above was extreme and dramatic but it is not unusual for students to value the support of the residences staff, who provide a flavour of home.

Housekeepers usually make routine checks on flats to ensure that communal areas are kept clean and tidy and that electrical appliances are limited to those permitted. During those visits they may come across other activities that give them cause for alarm.

Example: Mrs Anderson, the housekeeper, visited a flat for a routine check one Friday afternoon. She was examining a stain on the kitchen floor when one of the residents wandered into the kitchen, shrieked, then started to scream in a panicky way. She escorted him back to his room where two other students were lying on the floor looking dazed and glazed. These students were clearly not functioning normally and she guessed correctly that they had been experimenting with illegal drugs. She called the medical centre to ask for help and reported the incident to the manager of the residences, who subsequently took disciplinary action against the students involved.

The example given here is not unusual and presents a dilemma for all concerned. Drugs are illegal and clearly the students could be reported to the police. On the other hand, university staff often prefer to deal with the matter in house if possible in order to give the students a chance to change their behaviour. In this instance personal tutors may find themselves in a disciplinarian role while simultaneously helping students to understand the dangers of drugs.

We described above an instance where the student advice centre supported a student who lodged a complaint against a member of the academic staff. They are also sometimes involved in disputes concerning student residency.

Example: A group of students continually disregarded warnings about the amount of noise and mess they made in their flat. There were many complaints from other students and finally the manager of residences asked them to leave their flat. The students consulted the advice centre complaining of unfair treatment. The advice centre took up their case and confronted the manager of residences with the evidence. In this case the decision that had been taken to evict the students was upheld but there were tense moments between the two agencies while the battle was being fought.

While the supporting agencies of the university will need to work as a team in most instances there will be times, such as that described here, when it is important that students have someone to take up their case if they feel unfairly treated. Often it is the personal tutor who takes on this role. When this occurs it is vital that each case is examined individually and that generalizations about agencies, staff members and departments are avoided. There are usually two sides to every story and although it is tempting to cast one side into the role of the 'baddie' this is usually counter-productive. Residences are often seen in a poor light. There are abundant stories about all their faults and mistakes but as with most other things when all is well, and students' needs are met, it is 'non news' and goes unreported.

Chaplains

College chaplains have a much wider brief than tending to the needs of religious students. Although there is great variation in interpretation of this role it always includes a substantial element of pastoral care. Outgoing chaplains with a flexible outlook have contact with a broad spectrum of the student body, and have freedom to interact with students in interesting and creative ways. They often see themselves as having an informal role that enables them to drop in for coffee with groups of students or to take themselves to the Saturday night hop.

Chaplains are a valuable resource in an institution because they have a unique perspective on student life. They do not have a formal academic role nor do they run an agency that provides a welfare service. They have a formal role to administer religion to those who choose it and beyond that commitment there is time to spare to become involved in other things. For example, they may take it upon themselves to look out for particular groups of students, such as those from overseas, who may be lonely and disorientated.

Example: Lee Kok San was a bright and able young man from Hong Kong. However his spoken English was not good and he was very homesick. He attached himself to his personal tutor who was the only member of staff who had taken an interest in him, and began to call in regularly for a friendly chat. Lee Kok San had made no friends at university, partly because there were no other Chinese students on his course. The tutor mentioned the young man to the chaplain one day as he passed him on the campus, he immediately offered his help. The chaplain invited Lee to dinner at his home with a couple of other students that he knew, including a Chinese boy from another course. Lee made friends, first with the Chinese boy and in the course of time with the other students, following which he began to settle into his studies.

Chaplains are well placed to raise issues that are of general concern with the institutional authorities. Each department may have only one or two students belonging to a minority group but as chaplains meet the student body as a whole they are often able to identify the needs of a particular group across the university. For example a chaplain may take up the needs of overseas students and campaign for more resources to help them, such as an overseas students adviser.

There may be other events that affect student life that chaplains can confront, for example the arrival of an extreme religious sect recruiting vulnerable students on campus. They may try to tackle the problem at an institutional level, for instance by distributing warning leaflets or arranging to speak to a meeting of the students union. They may also be on hand to pick up the pieces when individuals are adversely affected.

Example: A religious organization targeted the university campus, looking for converts. Anna, a student who was shy and lonely, was approached by the sect who offered her the friendship and company she craved and she decided to become involved. Over the course of time the demands of the sect increased. They pressurized her to spend all her spare time recruiting new members and to make substantial financial contributions to the organization. She was stressed by the demands exerted on her and eventually consulted her tutor, who in turn referred her to the chaplain. The chaplain was able to help Anna rethink her religious beliefs, which resulted in her withdrawing from the sect. The chaplain supported her through a difficult time, dealing with the harassment of the sect and finding a new support system.

Extreme religious sects can have an especially powerful effect on vulnerable individuals such as students and adolescents. A common argument put forward is that their beliefs are the only truth, and a warning to converts that other people will say they are lunatics because they have been unable to find the truth themselves. Hence when other people do make this accusation it proves that this aspect of what they are saying is correct, therefore everything else must also be true. This is a forceful argument and one which often keeps students locked into the sect. In the example of Anna described above a lay person may have been able to help her but the added dimension of talking to a skilled and experienced religious person was effective in helping her sort out her beliefs.

It is difficult to imagine how an institution would handle tragedies without the presence of a chaplain. The death of a student or member of staff sends shock waves through an institution. The waves are particularly powerful at the epicentre of the crisis with those closest to the victim, but can resonate with others less closely involved. Rituals such as a memorial service can be a focus for the grieving process and provide an opportunity for those involved to say goodbye to their friend.

Example: A student was tragically killed in a house fire. Her fellow students from the course, her friends and lecturers were shocked and upset by her death. The chaplain spent time with her course group, arranged a memorial service for her, and was openly available for anyone to see her to talk through their experience of bereavement.

Chaplains are often approached for discussions about personal relationships. Universities are full of adolescents who are exploring their sexuality and developing a sexual identity. It is impossible to ignore sex as young people hug and kiss in public and are seen and sometimes heard to be sexually active in shared flats. Some students face conflicting demands from their desires and their church. The Catholic church opposes effective forms of birth control and considers abortion to be a sin, posing a dilemma for sexually active students of that faith.

Example: Elise was a French Catholic student on an exchange Erazmus programme. She became involved with an English student in her first term and found herself to be pregnant. Her personal tutor realized that something was wrong as she started to miss classes and appointments and arranged to see her. Elise told her tutor about the problem and after a long discussion with her, advised her to talk to the Catholic chaplain.

The chaplain, a woman, helped Elise to consider her options and offered her support whatever decision she took. Elise had the pregnancy terminated and continued to seek counselling from the chaplain, who in this instance was the right person to help her maintain her faith and resolve her conflicting feelings.

Overseas student adviser

In institutions which have a large proportion of overseas students there should ideally be someone designated to advise them. This person will probably provide overseas students with information about their arrival in Britain, the university they will be attending, the town in which they are situated and life in Britain, particularly about the weather! They may arrange an induction course, arrival ceremonies and some kind of befriending scheme or 'buddy' system. They will also be familiar with immigration regulations and be able to help and advise students about registration with the police and renewal of visas. The overseas student adviser may become involved with the families of students from abroad who often experience difficulties. They may also be called upon to help and advise students with specific exchange control regulations or other financial difficulties. This role and the problems experienced by overseas students have been discussed in detail in Chapter 7.

Departmental support systems

Departmental secretaries tend to know a considerable amount about the functioning of a department. Sensing this students often seek their advice about where to turn for help. The secretarial staff may be more approachable than academics. Students may choose to talk to other members of academic staff rather than their personal tutor. The tutorial system needs to be flexible enough for students to change tutor if they do not get on with the one allocated to them.

Physical recreation

Physical recreation departments of universities usually have something to offer everyone, from table tennis to volley ball or cricket to cross country running. Being involved in recreational activity has many benefits, physical, social, and psychological. Sport can be an excellent medium for becoming part of a group or a team. There may be times when encouragement to participate in some activity will be all that is needed to motivate a reluctant student lacking in friends and social life.

> *Example:* Nadim had been to see the student counsellor about feeling homesick, lonely and depressed. She listened to his concerns and asked him about his interests. She arranged to meet him for another session and in the meantime suggested that he take part in the weekend walks arranged by the physical recreation department. These gave him a chance to see some of the local countryside and meet other people in an informal manner. Nadim enjoyed his first walk and met an interesting group of people, one of whom later became a good friend.

Students union support systems

Many student unions operate a system of student support often called Niteline. This is a counselling agency run by volunteers which typically operates overnight, from 7.00 pm until 7.00 am. This and similar helplines are publicized widely among the student body. They aim to provide a listening ear for students with worries which emerge or become critical out of hours. Typically Niteline takes calls from students who are lonely or upset, who have taken drugs and are frightened of the effects, who have been drinking and have a depressed reaction to the alcohol, who are pregnant or want to know where the nearest contraceptive machine is, or who just want someone to talk to.

Disabled students advisory officer

Every university should have a person designated to advise disabled students and to represent their interests throughout the institution. This is both an advisory role and a political one. It is important that all departments are made aware of the needs of disabled students and that each one works towards making its courses as accessible as possible. Personal tutors who have disabled students amongst their tutees may find that they need support and guidance to ensure that all students have equal opportunities.

> *Example:* Lygia, a student studying music, had a hearing defect. She managed very well most of the time using her hearing aid although she had difficulty hearing in the large lecture theatres. Her personal tutor consulted the disabled students adviser who formally requested the installation of a loop system in the lecture theatre most frequently used by Lygia.

Disabled students are not always a high priority on the agenda of higher education colleges and sometimes tutors may have to use the formal channels described in Chapter 9 to ensure that the needs of such students are met.

External agencies

There are numerous agencies in every local community that can provide help or advice with specific problems. These include the Citizens Advice Bureau, Alcoholics Anonymous, Aquarius or other alcohol related agencies, Drugline, Aids Helpline, Friend, Gamblers Anonymous, Samaritans, as well as statutory agencies such as social services, probation and psychology services. Brief information about these agencies is given in the Appendix and their services may be made available through the student advice centre, the student counselling service or the medical centre.

Summary

The central message of this chapter is that personal tutors are not alone. It can be a daunting prospect to have responsibility for a dozen or so students with their numerous and varied worries and troubles. It is important to remember that there are other resources available to both tutors and students. The crucial element of the personal tutor's role is to get to know their students and develop a trusting relationship so that they are perceived to be a reliable port of call in a crisis. Patient listening enables a student to identify and share troubles, the other support services of the institution are able to offer their specialist skills if and when referrals are made. Team work and trust between the agencies of the university will enable students and staff to gain maximum benefit from the services provided.

9

The Process of Change in Higher Education

The effects of change

Teachers in higher education are currently subjected to many pressures due to changes in policy and practice imposed from both outside and inside their universities. These have been described at length earlier in this volume and include funding arrangements, teaching philosophy, student assessment, and the practice of research.

These changes in higher education have taken a toll on academic staff who have had to accommodate to them by making major adaptations. This has been, and continues to be, a source of stress. Change, or the prospect of it, is often perceived as a threatening process which induces powerful resistances in both individuals and groups. The threatening nature of this process is increased when individuals are required to make adjustments to their professional practice.

This chapter explores why individuals and organizations are resistant to change and offers a perspective from which tutors can develop a positive interaction with their institution. With a greater understanding of how the organization functions tutors will have more chance of playing an effective part by making useful contributions and consequently a lesser tendency to become frustrated, disillusioned, dispirited and eventually burned out. We propose that a model of interaction with an organization be adopted using principles derived from systems theory. We also outline the administrative structure of a typical university in order that tutors can attempt to make their interventions in an appropriate manner and place.

Personal tutors can act on the behalf of their students. In this role the academic has a responsibility to ensure that the welfare needs of students are met. This includes the provision of personal tutorials and facilitating students' use of the welfare network, which develop out of the interface of tutor–student contact. Tutors are also potential agents of change within the university. Through their contact with students they are able to identify shortcomings in welfare services and sometimes academic provision and can represent students' needs at the tutor–university interface. Tutors can develop an effective voice within the institution through which they can promote change. An awareness of the political process is an invaluable first step towards mobilizing it.

How people respond to change

The prospect of change often engenders anxiety. There is comfort in familiar, predictable routines and anything which threatens to disrupt them disturbs the individual. Change brings in its wake the prospect of uncertainty which in turn induces stress.

People differ in their reaction to anxiety generated by change and unfamiliar experiences. Some manage to contain the feelings of fear and anxiety and convert the experience into excitement, the high arousal being harnessed and used in a productive manner. Others are overwhelmed and feel helpless and hopeless, they are paralysed into a frozen state and collapse into a non-functioning mode, or run away. An analogy might be drawn between two children offered a ride on a ghost train at a fair-ground. Both would feel nervous and anxious; however one might regard this as a thrilling opportunity not to be missed at any cost, while the other would run a mile in the opposite direction, terrified that this experience will result in death or dismemberment.

These differing responses to anxiety are largely individually determined with some trends emerging. It may be useful to consider this from a psychodynamic perspective. When placed under duress our anxiety levels rise until they become unbearable. At this point, according to psychodynamic theory, psychological operations known as defence mechanisms come into play. These, as their name suggests, are intended to protect us from the effects of anxiety. A further effect is that defences tend to mitigate against the process of change. They are unconsciously activated, which means they come into play automatically, often without the individual being aware that they are occurring.

Psychological defences take a number of forms. A common one is denial, where feelings are pushed away or cut off.

Example: A fortnight before her finals Sybil decided to take a holiday. She told her friends she was going climbing in Scotland and would return in time for the exams. They knew that this behaviour was uncharacteristic of her and attempted to persuade her to stay. In response Sybil said she had done enough preparation and was not worried about her performance.

Here Sybil was denying her worries about finals. She was a conscientious student who had worked consistently well throughout the course and was expected to gain a good degree. Facing the hurdle of finals was too much for her and she cut off from the overwhelming anxiety engendered by this impending deadline.

Sybil's friends persuaded her to postpone her decision and arrange an appointment with her tutor. In the intervening period she realized the mistake she was making and decided to stay and study for her exams.

Example: Toby was a lecturer with three years experience and no publications. During an appraisal exercise he was informed that the university expected him to write two articles within the next year, failure to do so would result in certain dismissal. When asked how he was getting on with this task he claimed it was going well, however at the end of the year he had written nothing. He was asked to leave.

Toby had difficulty writing, he much preferred teaching. His anxiety about putting pen to paper proved to be insurmountable. He was unable to face the challenge and instead became cut off from both the task he was asked to execute and the potential consequences, in this he was exhibiting a defence of denial.

It is important to differentiate between decisions which are reached after careful consideration and those which are made without conscious awareness.

Example: A colleague of Toby's left the university. He enjoyed teaching but felt research was not for him. After discussing his options he made a decision to leave and found a new post before handing in his notice.

This lecturer made a positive, conscious decision to leave. Unlike Toby he thought about the issues, considered his position and explored other possibilities. He left at a time which suited him and moved on to alternative employment. He did not exhibit defensive responses.

A further defence mechanism is known as projection. In this the person does not take responsibility for the part they have played; instead others are assigned the blame.

Example: Following his dismissal Toby was angry with his head of department and launched an appeal against the decision. He said he was a dedicated academic who was well liked by the students and did not see why he should leave. He felt that he had been persecuted and sacked unfairly, without warning. During his appraisal he had undertaken to write two articles and had signed the report which stated he agreed with the recommendations of his senior colleague. Despite this he was unable to accept any level of responsibility for his failure and held the head of department entirely to blame.

Example: Gerald was a senior lecturer of many years standing. He found difficulty adapting to the changes in expectations and behaviour of his students. In his day students had not questioned the authority of academics, they had listened politely and taken notes. Now he found that there were constant interruptions as students posed questions in tutorials. Every coffee break he was to be found in the staff room pacing up and down in an agitated and angry frame of mind, complaining about 'the students of today' to whoever would listen.

Gerald had worked for many years in the same university and initially had led a settled existence with little disruption or change to contend with. Now, as change was imposed from the university, he was increasingly unable to cope. Instead of either reflecting on his personal difficulty or challenging the university authorities, he blamed the students. To him they were unpredictable, rude and demanding. Despite discussions with colleagues, who attempted to explain that students were encouraged to pose questions with a new philosophy of active participation in learning, he continued to hold this view. He was unable to either recognize or accept his responsibility for adapting to changed expectations.

We have described two defences which are a common reaction to anxiety generated by change or unfamiliarity. There are many other forms of defence, all of which operate automatically. They have a protective function in the short term, in that they shield the person from incapacitating anxiety, but when they are maintained over long periods they are almost always counter-productive. For instance Sybil needed temporary escape from her panicky feelings about her finals. When she allowed herself time to consider whether her proposed holiday was wise she realized that she wanted to take her exams and perform well in them. To do this she needed to revise and set herself a structured study programme. Her anxiety level and defences came down sufficiently for her to face the reality of her situation and weigh up her priorities. As a consequence she successfully completed her exams.

Toby and Gerald did not have the capacity to face the realities of the demands on them. Toby pushed his worries aside and as a result did not act to safeguard his future. Gerald battled on in a chronically dissatisfied and increasingly uncomfortable role.

A further impact demonstrated in these examples is that defences can act against the process of change. For both Toby and Gerald defences were perhaps effective in the short term but when employed over a prolonged period they proved to be disabling, as they hindered resolution of the underlying problems. Here defences prevented confrontation with reality and thereby blocked any adaptations which could be made.

Anxiety is often stimulated by the prospect of an unfamiliar task. In higher education the challenges faced by newly appointed and established members of staff are different. For the newly appointed lecturer anxiety is often provoked by having to teach, speaking to a large group of students in a lecture theatre, leading a seminar, or conducting a tutorial. After a number of repetitions these duties become more familiar and hence less threatening. As with any task experience and practice help to increase confidence, in response anxiety decreases and gradually mastery of the task is accomplished.

Senior academics are usually well established and confident in a teaching role. For this group of staff anxiety is more commonly generated in response to changes in the curriculum or the introduction of new teaching methods. Adapting to such changes tends to be more difficult than for new lecturers because experienced teachers first have to go through a process of deskilling, followed by a gradual redevelopment of skills. For example let us consider the introduction of student directed teaching in which small group seminars are central. In these the seminar leader has a role which is relatively non-directive and facilitative. This contrasts with lecturing, the traditional university teaching mode, where a more didactic style is adopted. The change from lectures to small group seminars involves a major transition, both in the philosophy and skills required. Similarly the recent increase in student numbers, which has led to a reduction in the incidence of small group seminars and greatly increased lecture audiences, is challenging academics once again to examine their teaching methods.

Groups and change

We have outlined ways in which individuals respond to the stress of change and how they bring defensive processes into operation in order to protect themselves against the fear engendered by uncertainty. In a similar manner groups of people react against change by mounting defensive processes and resistances.

Group interactions have been studied in depth by numerous writers from psychoanalysts to sociologists. A useful concept to emerge from this is the description by Elliot Jaques (1955) of social defence systems. He postulates that these are similar to individual psychological defences but are characteristic of groups. They are based on the same principle, derived from observation studies, that real or potential change stirs up deep anxiety which in turn acts to prevent change from occurring. As with individual defences these social defence systems function at an unconscious level and automatically come into operation on exposure to threat. The group resistance to change is greater than individual responses would suggest and increases with the size of the group.

As people we all exist in groups and take part in social processes. Within organizations there are numerous social and work groups which form a complex network of interrelated and overlapping systems. Studies such as those conducted by Bion (1961) have shed light on the internal mechanisms which act in groups. He described two categories which he called work groups and basic assumption groups. All groups tend to shift between work, when the task assigned is being closely adhered to, and a non-working state when a basic assumption is operative. Bion further divides these non-working states into three types reflecting the prominent behaviour of the group as a whole. They are dependency, pairing, and fight-flight, which are in effect three forms of group defensive operations.

Example: A working party was set up to explore the potential for introducing a staff room in a department. It seemed to get off to a good start and there was considerable enthusiasm and sharing of ideas in the group. Early in the series of arranged meetings a new member of staff, Harold, joined the group. Harold was enthusiastic and vocal and in discussion he expressed his views forcefully. Over a short space of time he became dominant within the group as the other members fell silent. Their initial enthusiasm appeared to evaporate and they made no further significant contributions. Eventually several people stopped attending the meetings and the proposal was abandoned.

Here an effective working group was threatened by a new, dominant member. The group as a whole responded by looking to Harold for direction, thus they adopted a defensive position of dependency in which work was no longer occurring. Instead one person's voice came to represent all their views. Over a period of time the group as a whole became redundant and adopted a flight response, they stopped attending. The group no longer functioned, in fact it no longer existed. The initially promising work disintegrated and the final outcome was that the group failed to complete the task it set out to achieve.

The working capacity of a group is affected by factors such as size, task assigned and leadership structure. Small groups tend to be more efficient and able to stick to the task. Obholtzer (1989) suggests a critical factor in determining the maximum effective group size is the capacity to maintain eye contact with all members of the group. This is possible in groups of up to twelve members, above this number the group is more likely to fall into a defensive mode of operation. Translating this into committee work a useful rule of thumb is that meetings with up to twelve members are likely to be productive and able to stick to the task. When membership exceeds twelve the meeting is most probably best viewed as a place where information can be disseminated.

Clarity about structure and leadership tends to increase the work capacity of groups. Leadership here refers not to the imposition of control, which would encourage the group to become dependent and non-working as in the example of Harold, but rather that an individual within the group takes responsibility for ensuring that the group sticks to the task. This role might be more accurately described as a facilitator. Structure includes attention to the membership and aims of a group, promotion of both these factors enhances effective work. Part of the role of a chairperson is to convene a meeting and to ensure that the membership is appropriate to the task in hand.

The process of change is uncomfortable for both individuals and organizations. This process can be facilitated by consultation, in which people feel they are involved in the decision-making process. The style of leadership is crucial as is the structure of the organization. For instance, as described above, the membership of working groups with a brief to develop and initiate policies is best limited to a small number, certainly not greater than twelve. It should be remembered that however well change is managed there will be casualties, individuals such as Gerald who are unable to adapt to new expectations. We shall proceed to outline a model of intervention which is often useful when major resistance to change is encountered, either in an individual or a group.

A systems perspective of change

In the previous section we have described the incapacitating effects of anxiety, defensive processes which are mounted to protect both individuals and groups from anxiety, and resistances which counteract proposed change.

A common adverse effect of change imposed by external sources is that individuals often feel helpless and frustrated by their powerlessness when they attempt to influence the institution. In the worst possible scenario they launch repetitive but ineffectual attacks on the organization which does not respond. Thus a vicious cycle is set up in which the battling individual is eventually reduced to a demoralized and exhausted state. In parallel with this the institution becomes weary of the process of consultation, which it perceives as counter-productive. It then becomes more autocratic, either imposing changes without consultation or paying lip service to the process.

Example: Pauline was an academic who believed that students were given a raw deal by the university. She thought that there should be an increase in welfare provision and time made available for personal tutorials. In discussions with students she often raised this issue and the majority agreed. Pauline became increasingly angry with the university for not providing more pastoral care. She often talked about her concerns and as a consequence other staff became irritated with her. This indicated to Pauline that they were not sympathetic to her views which further fuelled her anger. Eventually communication broke down, Pauline became isolated and alienated and her campaign had less and less impact.

Using a concept from systems theory this deadlocked situation would be viewed as an example of a closed system. In this state energy is used unproductively and change is not possible. Pauline was exhausting herself to no avail. Although she was attempting to induce changes her efforts were misdirected and therefore fruitless. She was becoming burned out and ultimately was unable to help either her students, her colleagues, or herself.

A more effectual organization would harness the energy of its individual staff members and thereby promote change and growth, in other words it would operate as an open system. Applying this model we argue that a closed system is dysfunctional, whereas an open system is functional. The concept of systems theory has been developed into a tool which is widely used in family therapy (Burnham, 1986). We propose that it can also be applied within organizations. From the perspective of tutors this can provide a framework for understanding the way the system functions and how they might interact with it more effectively. We will expand this further by presenting a description of systems theory followed by examples of dysfunctional and functional systems.

Figure 9.1 An open system

Figure 9.2 A closed system

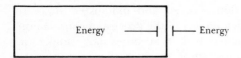

Systems theory

Systems theory takes as its starting point the central tenet that 'the whole is greater than the sum of its parts' (Von Bertalanffy, 1968). The 'whole' here consists of a system of interconnecting and interacting smaller units which are contained by a boundary. A distinction is made between open and closed systems, the former being 'the basis of fundamental life phenomena' (Von Bertalanffy, 1969).

In this model an open system is in constant dynamic equilibrium with the surrounding environment, separated by a permeable boundary across which energy is transported. Within the system energy is utilized, transformed, and then exported out of the system, as illustrated in Figure 9.1. Examples of open systems range from an individual human cell to a Universe and encompass organizations including universities.

A closed system, in contrast, is independent of its environment and reaches a steady state through chemical equilibria contained within it. A closed system is surrounded by a fixed, impenetrable boundary. It cannot be energized and produces a limited amount of work following which it becomes exhausted, or dead, as in Figure 9.2. An example is an electrical system powered by a battery which ultimately runs flat because the energy it contains is finite.

Within a university students and staff relate in a number of social and working groups. These form a complex network of interrelated and overlapping systems. Some of these systems are relatively closed, others are open. The university contains a number of open systems in its boundary, some systems also extend beyond this as networks may be composed of elements both from within and outside the university.

We propose a model which postulates that problems arise in universities when systems become closed. In this state small, dysfunctional systems are set up which are not in a dynamic interaction with other systems. Instead they exist independently of their environment, closed off and unable to benefit from the exchange of energy. No dialogue is possible and productive work cannot be achieved. The closed system is surrounded by an impenetrable wall and will eventually grind to a halt as its energy reserves are exhausted.

The impasse which developed between Pauline and her colleagues is an example. Here Pauline became a closed system, she was unable to have an effective interaction with the university but kept trying. Over the course of time barriers were erected between Pauline and her colleagues which eventually became impenetrable. Meanwhile Pauline became exhausted and demoralized and began to burn out.

Taking this model as a starting place it is possible to develop ideas about useful interventions. The essential task for the tutor is to identify when closed systems are in existence, then to facilitate their conversion to open systems. When this occurs the system is converted from lifeless to living, or dysfunctional to functional. The tutor's role within the institution can be viewed as an agent of change who assists the development of energy exchange. Acting from this perspective may enable the tutor to develop an influential relationship with the larger systems of the organization. We will proceed to expand on these themes in the following section.

Identifying closed systems

Closed systems can operate at many levels. A person can exist to an extent as a closed system, a hermit being the classic example of an individual who has withdrawn from society. In contrast most of us interact with our environment in an open manner, to a greater or lesser extent. We all require food and water and other basic necessities, although individuals have differing levels of social interaction.

The individual as a system

Example: Cathy came to see her tutor at his request. She failed to attend a series of seminars in her first term and the tutor wondered why. She arrived punctually for the appointment, came into the room, sat down and was silent. Cathy looked at the floor, avoiding eye contact and sat in a hunched posture with arms crossed, shoulders forward, and knees tightly squeezed together. The tutor felt uncomfortable and the tension in the room was almost palpable.

From a systems perspective we would say that Cathy was functioning as a closed system. She was presenting herself as an insular person with a prominent boundary between her inner thoughts and the tutor. Her non-verbal behaviour is telling the tutor to keep away, she makes no contact with her eyes and her arms and legs form a protective barrier reinforcing this message.

The tutor recognized the signals and responded to them. Cathy was clearly not going to open up to him easily. Given her level of discomfort it had taken her an immense effort of will to get to the meeting. Realizing he was likely to make the situation worse if he questioned Cathy he decided instead to comment on her obvious discomfort in an empathic manner. He said, 'Thank you for coming today. I invited you along because I was worried and wondered why I hadn't seen you at the tutorials. I can see that you feel uncomfortable in here and you're finding it difficult to talk.'

In his intervention the tutor was attempting to give Cathy the opportunity to open up to him. He wanted to develop a dialogue, to understand her problems. To do this it was necessary to take down the barrier which separated Cathy from him. He was sensitive to her need to protect herself and to her right to privacy. Only Cathy could decide whether to share her troubles by talking to the tutor.

Cathy took a deep breath and began to talk, initially with great hesitancy but gathering momentum as she continued. As she spoke she became visibly more relaxed, sat back in her chair, uncrossed her arms and managed to make eye contact with the tutor. From being in a closed off and isolated position she shared her problems, and in the process the closed system which she had been trapped in became open. There was communication with the tutor. Once he grasped her difficulties he was able to offer support and advice which Cathy felt able to take. As her system opened up she became energized instead of paralysed.

A group as a closed system
Groups can also operate as closed systems. Some communities are relatively isolated, perhaps geographically or because they have made an active choice to withdraw from mainstream society. Examples of the latter include many religious communities which create an external boundary in order to allow a protected internal space to develop.

Within universities closed groups can indicate systemic dysfunction. They are usually identified by the existence of a deadlock situation. The example of Harold joining a working group described above illustrates this. Here a newcomer tipped the balance from an effective to a non-functional group. Harold was split off and isolated from the other members of the group, who withdrew from contact with him. There was a breakdown in communication and two closed systems, Harold and the group, emerged.

In this instance the presence of a facilitating chairperson may have prevented his arrival from being so devastating. A central part of this role is to facilitate communication within the group. Here the chairperson would listen to Harold's contribution and then invite comments from other members. If Harold continued to speak the chairperson would ask him to await his turn, stressing that it was also important to take into consideration alternative points of view.

An organization can sometimes operate as a large, closed group. This was Pauline's experience of her university. She was concerned about the lack of welfare provision for students and rightly began to consult colleagues and students to ascertain whether they shared her views. However, once she tried to effect change in the organization she met with what seemed to her an impenetrable brick wall, no one was prepared to take action.

In Pauline's case she was ineffective because she did not know how and where to direct her efforts. Within her university there was a committee responsible for student welfare. Pauline was unaware of the existence of this committee, neither did her colleagues seem to know about it. Here Pauline as an individual had become closed off and isolated. The university had also effectively closed off an important avenue of communication by not making its staff aware of this formal structure. Thus the university was not harnessing the energy and ideas of the staff members to the detriment of the organization, its staff and students.

This example highlights the importance of tutors knowing how to interact with their institutions and where to target their efforts. Universities should take a lead in informing their employees and students about the administrative structure, unless this occurs they deprive themselves of valuable feedback. In order that an effective working alliance can develop staff and students need to know where to make comments and how to represent their views.

The administrative structure of a university

In this section we present a model of the administrative structure within a university. The purpose of this is to give tutors a basis from which to explore the institution they work in. With this awareness they are more likely to be able to interact productively with the administration and therefore be politically effective.

In an ideal university the administrative structure should operate as an open system, interacting with and responding to the concerns of individuals and groups. All too often this does not occur and committees are composed of a restricted number of powerful individuals who may not be aware of the problems experienced at grass roots level. The frustrations encountered by Pauline, described earlier, are an example of this. Further consequences of lack of consultation are that decisions which directly affect individuals can be made without full consideration of their impact.

Example: At the beginning of his second year Robin went to see his tutor to explain that he would be withdrawing from his part-time master's degree course. He was a successful and interested student and, in response to the tutor questioning his decision, he explained that he could not afford to continue. He had taken out a loan to pay the fees, which at the time he commenced the course were £2000 per

Figure 9.3   The administrative structure of a model university

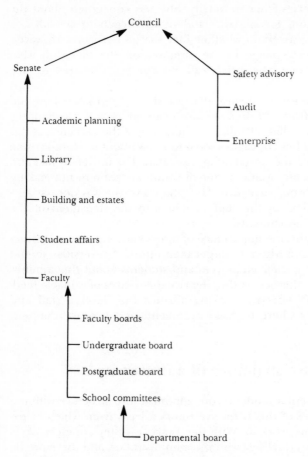

annum. A decision to increase the fees by 50 per cent had been taken and was to be applied with immediate effect, therefore he was required to pay £3000 for the second year. Because he was unable to raise a further loan he left without obtaining his degree.

This example illustrates the difficulties created by a limited vision which considers only one aspect of a problem, in this case the financial position of the university. In effect the students were required to cover a budgetary shortfall. This in turn posed a problem for tutors within that department as many students faced the same dilemma. It is relatively easy for administrators to make such a decision as they are distant from the individual students who suffer the consequences. Had the tutors been involved in discussions it is likely that they would have anticipated this situation, as they were aware of the financial struggles of their students. In this case an alternative strategy could then have been developed.

University committees

No two universities are identical with respect to their administration and structure. It is therefore important that tutors find out how their particular institution operates and direct their interaction appropriately. Given that there is great individual variation we have attempted to construct a model of university administration which will guide tutors and help them develop signposts to their own university. This is presented in Figure 9.3.

As can be seen from the diagram there is a complex system of committees which operates in a hierarchical fashion with information and decision-making being processed up and down the chain. Officially communication passes through the committees via formal channels and it is important that tutors know how these operate. It is also helpful to become familiar with the identities of key figures who are represented throughout the hierarchy as they facilitate the linking process between committees.

In any political structure formal approaches to committees are augmented by informal groups and liaison at outside meetings. An effective chairperson is usually one who welcomes such contact and can channel concerns in an appropriate direction.

Council
The university council is the body which oversees all administrative functions of the university. It holds overall financial responsibility and is the central policy making body. It is composed of lay, academic and, sometimes, student representatives and therefore provides a vehicle for the interaction between the university, its internal population of students and staff, and the external population it serves. In Scottish universities there is an elected rector, commonly an individual in the public eye. The Senate, the committee directly answerable to council, is also represented.

Senate
The purpose of the senate is to keep under continuous review the academic development of the university. All academic departments therefore report to senate, which in turn reports to council. The size and composition of the senate varies greatly. In the Open University all academic staff have a place in the senate. In other universities it is composed of representatives from the groups directly reporting to it, plus deans, pro-vice chancellors, vice chancellors, and elected representatives from faculties.

In our model there are five subcommittees directly reporting to the senate: academic planning; library; building and estates; student affairs; and faculties.

Academic planning
This body monitors the content of existing degrees and considers proposals for the introduction of new courses. It is composed of senior academic staff and nominated representatives of each faculty board.

Library
This subcommittee is responsible for running library facilities, including the purchase of books and journals for which it has a budget.

Building and estates
As its name suggests the purpose of this group is to maintain, plan and build university facilities. It also has a remit to monitor the use of space and make recommendations accordingly. This committee may be linked laterally to the safety executive, in addition both are required to conform to statutory external regulations.

Student affairs
For the tutor this subcommittee is central as it co-ordinates matters relating to student welfare. In our model university this body represents the welfare interests of students at senate. Therefore any issues pertaining to personal tutoring are discussed here and policies for personal tutors and welfare issues are developed. Before being ratified they are presented at senate.

The student affairs group consists of members from welfare, student counselling, tutors, and students. Together they identify problems and deficiencies within this service which are either presented directly to senate, or alternatively used to develop proposals for change, which are in turn considered by senate. A personal tutor's group, although not included in the administrative structure, would have members on student affairs, therefore issues of concern would be taken up formally through this channel.

In the example of Pauline this group would be the optimum place for her concerns to be raised. As well as promoting consideration of the problem and potential remedial action Pauline would have gained the support of colleagues also interested in student welfare, thus decreasing her isolation and sense of alienation. Via this group she would have been able to open and thereby free up her internal, exhausted, system and that of the university.

Faculty
The faculties are one of the main channels through which academic activities are represented at senate. In our model the subcommittees represented at faculty are: faculty board; undergraduate board; postgraduate board; and schools. Departments report to faculty via their schools. Where there are no schools within a university, departments usually report direct to faculty. There is a dean of faculty who is usually an elected member but may be appointed by the vice chancellor.

An illustration of the decision-making process within this administrative machinery gives an insight into its operation.

> *Example:* A member of staff in a department considered the potential for introducing a new course. She discussed this informally with several colleagues and gained a general feeling of support plus some further suggestions. She then consulted the head of department, who

recommended she submit an outline plan to the next departmental board meeting. This she did, incorporating suggestions from her peers into the written proposal.

After discussion the document was modified and subsequently submitted first to the school committee, then faculty, then the senate. These were moves up the hierarchy. From the senate academic planning were directed to consider the proposal and, following a few modifications, recommended it be accepted. This was reported back to the senate, who formally adopted the proposal. This was then reported to council in the senate minutes.

Example: In Chapter 1 we described Joanne, who thought she was being followed by an intruder on campus. Her tutor took up her concerns directly with her, as well as taking action within the university. The outcome of this was that improved street lighting was installed and regular security patrols were instigated.

Joanne's tutor contacted the counselling service at the university. Without revealing her identity he spoke about the incident and his concerns, not just for this student but also for others. The counselling staff had encountered a number of worried students and the stimulus of the tutor's enquiry prompted them to discuss the situation at their next meeting. After discussion it was decided to put security on the agenda of the next student affairs committee, who made a recommendation to senate. The senate reported to the council, who directed both the safety advisory and buildings and estates committees simultaneously to consider safety on campus. Recommendations were made to the council who ordered their implementation.

Here a problem initially raised informally became formalized and was presented to the appropriate committee within the organization. This was taken up the hierarchy to the council, who then referred it back to two committees within different arms of the administration for their expert consideration. Action was taken because the tutor catalysed a parallel concern within the student counselling service. As this group was represented on student affairs they raised the issue of security as a matter of urgency. Action was expedited to ensure the safety of students and staff and to protect the reputation of the university. Taken from the systems perspective we might say that the system was already partly open, represented by the level of anxiety. The informal contact, as is often the case, proved to be the trigger opening event.

Summary

A knowledge of the political process can greatly enhance the tutor's interaction with the university to the benefit of students, staff and the overall functioning of the organization. In this chapter we have explored the process of change, examined some of the difficulties encountered, and outlined how a systems viewpoint can facilitate this process. Understanding the structure of an organization is an essential first step to developing effective communication and the model of university administration presented is designed to help personal tutors begin this interaction. Formal consultation within institutions is often instigated by informal discussion therefore we suggest that tutors play an active role in exploring their concerns and ideas with others, thus opening these systems of communication and building alliances.

Sometimes it may be necessary to mobilize support from elsewhere, for instance by taking advice from professional, social or legal representatives who operate outside the university. They can add specialist knowledge which in effect opens the system to change using additional powers of persuasion. An example is the health and safety legislation which sets down minimum acceptable standards and can be used to protect the interests of students and staff.

It is important that tutors view themselves as potential agents of change. Through contact with their students they are in an ideal position to recognize problem areas and take these up within the university, as described in the case of Joanne. Tutors can thus stimulate open communication between the university and its students.

10

Summary and Resources for Personal Tutors

This book is intended to act as a practical guide for personal tutors working in higher education. In the foregoing chapters we have described the multiple roles played by personal tutors, outlined some basic counselling skills, given an introduction to the problems of adolescent development, difficulties encountered with academic work and placed emphasis on populations with increased vulnerability, including overseas, postgraduate and mature students. We have also paid attention to issues confronting all those who work within institutions who wish to influence wider working practices. It is hoped that personal tutors, as a result of being armed with this information, will be able to function more effectively and efficiently in their role than would otherwise be the case.

This, the final chapter, aims to take the process further by focusing attention on the resources required to fulfil the role of personal tutor. Current trends in higher education are towards increasing student enrolment without a corresponding increase in academic staff, therefore the pressure on personal tutors will inevitably rise. Some welfare resources will of necessity be provided by other areas of the institution. In this chapter attention is paid to ways of facilitating links with other people involved in this work. Suggestions for organizing time and training requirements are made. We also highlight the importance of tutors looking after their own needs, a much neglected topic.

Developing the skills required to become an effective personal tutor involves a learning process which takes time. For most personal tutors these skills are gradually acquired with increasing experience. Problems are encountered, are tackled as they occur, and learning takes place from within the role.

In earlier chapters we have given examples of a variety of difficulties and have focused on common themes which emerge in student lives. We have described how these difficulties were explored and, in many instances, successfully resolved. However it would be impossible to prepare the tutor for all eventualities, indeed to attempt to do so would be a disservice to the student and tutor, as in many cases there is no easily applied formula for resolution. We view it as more useful for tutors to develop the capacity to work within their limits, to know when they need help, or when it is appropriate to suggest an alternative resource for a student in difficulty. This latter route is not an admission of failure on the part of the tutor, it is rather an acknowledgement of the wide range of resources and specialist knowledge available elsewhere, both within and outside the university.

When encountering a new situation a great deal of benefit can come out of reflecting on the problem presented. Tutors may feel anxious and out of their depth, or alternatively may be able to relate to the student and problem to some extent. The stronger the feelings of uncertainty and unfamiliarity, the more likelihood there is that expert advice is required. Therefore it is often fruitful for tutors to be aware of their own level of anxiety.

Links with other personal tutors

The central danger which many personal tutors face is isolation. Tutors working without support commonly encounter a number of difficulties. They tend to overestimate the scope of work expected of them, and with it their own capacity to provide a realistic level of help for individual students. They can become anxious about the responsibilities of tutoring. Tutors are often dealing with anxious students and some of this anxiety may be picked up by the tutor. When this is not shared tutors tend to develop an increasing level of discomfort which eventually fosters resentment at the heavy responsibility carried and, ultimately, even anger with the students seeking help. This is counter-productive for students, tutors, and the university. It is therefore important for tutors to consider ways in which isolation can be reduced and sharing of problems increased.

One way of avoiding isolation is for personal tutors to meet other tutors. This may sound easier than it actually is. Assistance can usually be obtained from the head of department, or via a senior academic who co-ordinates welfare services, or through a student counselling agency.

Once other tutors have been identified it can be useful to consult them about tutorial work. Personal contacts may be as helpful as the welfare services in a time of crisis. Sometimes personal tutors will find a mentor who is willing to talk in confidence about problems encountered. This support can be invaluable, especially if problems are anticipated and discussed before the tutor has a major predicament to deal with. There is usually some warning of impending crises which may then be averted. In such discussions, as pointed out earlier, individual students need not be named or identified, thereby preserving confidentiality.

> *Example:* Abid popped in to see his tutor three days running. Each time he spoke briefly about a minor difficulty then, without giving the tutor a chance to respond, made a rapid exit. The tutor mentioned this to a colleague who reminded her that Abid had failed a

previous examination. The tutor realized that Abid was probably very anxious about the coming exams. She then made an appointment to see him and warned him in advance that they would need at least half an hour. This ensured that Abid could not rush off without having a reasonable amount of time to talk through his problems.

When they met it emerged that Abid was extremely anxious about taking exams. He had in the past panicked and walked out of an important assessment which resulted in his having to resit. He was deeply ashamed of this behaviour and of his failure. He was also aware of the tutor's busy timetable and did not wish to be a nuisance, which explained why he had terminated the previous meetings so abruptly. The tutor arranged for him to attend a series of anxiety management sessions at the counselling centre where he was helped to deal with his anxiety more effectively. He subsequently successfully completed his exams.

Here the tutor was absolutely correct in her suspicion that there was something wrong. She sensed Abid's anxiety by feeling anxious herself. Talking to a colleague helped her to realize what was going on. By following her intuition and taking anticipatory action she was able to instigate help at a time when it could be used. Had she waited it is likely that Abid's anxiety would have escalated and prevented him from working effectively. A crisis could then have ensued either during the exams, when he might have walked out, or at the time of the results, if he failed. Abid was spared considerable distress and a further experience of failure, which would have rocked his fragile sense of self-esteem. Of course we cannot be certain of the outcome had the tutor not intervened but here her action had clearly been helpful to the student.

A further advantage in this instance was that had Abid failed his exams the tutor may have needed to spend a considerable amount of time with him during the summer months, giving extra tuition. Instead the tutor was able to concentrate on her research. Thus the intervention was not only a success but also an economical use of time for both student and tutor. From the perspective of the university the effect was also positive. A likely failure was turned into a success and the tutor's research programme continued without further interruption from Abid.

Groups for personal tutors

In addition to informal links with tutors there may be a formal network operating. In some universities there are regular, usually termly, meetings of personal tutors which provide a forum for tutors to meet and discuss common problems. These are often held within departments with a senior tutor acting as co-ordinator. To ensure that these groups function well their size should be restricted to about twelve members, therefore in large de-partments there may be several established. Tutors are encouraged to bring along difficult examples or dilemmas about tutoring and open discussion, with a sharing of ideas, information, and experiences, ensues.

An alternative model of a group for personal tutors is more highly structured. This may take the form of a series of meetings focusing on common difficulties encountered, for instance exploration of the problems of first year students. Here a number of tutors contribute their experiences and information about a specific theme. These meetings can be enhanced by involving members of the welfare team to provide specialist input.

There are many ways in which groups of personal tutors can operate and advantages and disadvantages in both examples described. The open group offers a more immediate source of help for tutors facing particular problems, however unless it has a facilitator discussion may become very loose and unfocused. The structured group may become overly directed and so lose a sense of spontaneity and aliveness. Overall the most effective form of the group is probably determined by the needs of its members.

When a group for personal tutors exists it will require, as do most groups, a co-ordinator to help it to function effectively. It is the responsibility of the co-ordinator to notify members about meetings. A facilitator is also useful, it is their task to conduct the meetings, to keep a balance between open and focused discussion, and to encourage contributions.

Training courses for personal tutors are addressed in a following section, these often incorporate larger meetings where the student welfare team speak about their services. This is helpful to tutors who can benefit from their experience, put names to faces, and begin to get an overall picture of the resources available.

Through this network the tutor can also keep abreast of new developments and form part of a collective strategy to influence change. The tutor, because of regular contact with students, is in an ideal position to identify problems and therefore promote remedial action. As was explored earlier in this volume the group will need to have an official voice within the university in order for change to be effected by it and through it. In an ideal world a helpful response will be promoted by going through formal channels of communication.

Women as personal tutors

It is no accident that when a network of personal tutors has been established the regular participants are often women. There are a number of reasons for this. First, women traditionally occupy a caring role in society therefore there is an assumption that they will do likewise in an institution. There is a widely held belief that this type of work is better done by women. Comments such as 'women are well suited to it', 'students prefer to talk to them', 'it is the sort of thing that comes naturally to women', are often heard. There is no direct evidence to support this assumption but it probably holds true as a generalization that women tend to be better listeners than men.

One problem propagated by this stance is that young women academics developing their careers may invest considerable time and effort in this role. Despite increased attention being paid to equal opportunities the majority of senior academic staff are male. It follows that personal tutoring is not directly linked to promotion opportunities and in fact it is sadly thought to be a relatively unimportant role in many universities.

A second and more sinister reason for the majority of personal tutors being women may therefore be based on an underlying assumption that 'men have got more important things to do with their time'.

Allocation of time for personal tutoring

It can prove difficult to limit the time allocated to personal tutorials. However this constitutes only part of an academic role and time boundaries should be established in order that other work can be protected. There is a danger to young academics, whether male or female, in investing heavily in a task which may not be valued by senior colleagues, which is demanding, and which can be very time consuming. Other work, more likely to lead to career progression, may be cast aside in the face of immediate demands from students in distress. It is difficult to say no, especially when the student has come knocking at the door, even though the tutor will have to make up for the lost working time later that evening.

These points are being put forward in order to reinforce the importance of tutors looking after their own interests and needs. Personal tutoring is for the most part a very rewarding and enjoyable activity and through it academics gain personal contact with students which is not possible in the lecture room. It is likely to be even more rewarding if potential pitfalls are seen in advance and are then successfully negotiated.

One of the tasks to be confronted by the personal tutor is to establish the role in a formal capacity. It is essential that this role is recognized to be an important and valuable contribution to the institution, and to the department. A crucial step towards recognition is the allocation of time.

We suggest that for a tutor with fifteen tutees the time allocated should be a minimum of two hours per week. There is also a case to be made for certain student groups who may be more demanding of their personal tutors to have an additional time allowance. This could include some overseas and mature students.

Having established this time officially it is important to use it well. Other work, including research time, should be preserved. Although some academics can readily return to work following an interruption this is not true for everyone. The style of tutoring should be determined by the tutor's own needs, balanced against the necessity of being available and accessible to students. Remember that sacrificing your own career is not a good example to the student, neither is it likely to help future student groups.

Drop-in session

A model of practice successfully adopted by many tutors is based on the notion of a drop-in session. In this tutors take a specific day and time of the week to see students. This system can operate with or without appointments. Ideally there should be a secretary to take calls from students, especially if appointments are given. This is not always possible but alternative arrangements can be made, bearing in mind the need for confidentiality. An example is that a tutor may display a list of available appointment times on a noticeboard and students sign up to claim a slot. When tutors routinely see all students the need for confidentiality about appointment time is negligible. If a student has specifically requested a meeting they may not wish to broadcast this fact and this system can be adapted in a coded form. In this the student writes 'taken' beside an available time, and leaves their name in a confidential note for the tutor.

This model has the advantage that it protects time not assigned to the task of tutoring therefore minimizes the disruption to tutors' timetables. It also ensures that tutoring takes priority for a specific time each week and for the most part is sufficient for students' requirements. One disadvantage is that in a crisis the student may have to wait a few days to be seen. It is therefore advisable to ensure students are well informed about sources of help which are more immediately available, such as phone lines or a counselling service. An introductory booklet for students joining the university can include this information. It is usefully reinforced by the personal tutor, perhaps in a talk to their group of tutees early during the course. Further information can be publicized at strategic points on campus and in departments. When secretaries take calls from students they should be briefed about alternative sources of help.

Training for personal tutors

Training in the skills of personal tutoring is highly desirable. We recommend that all tutors should attend a brief training course prior to taking up their duties. This introductory training should then be followed up by refresher courses.

Most universities have a staff development centre which organizes training courses although the emphasis placed on personal tutoring varies between institutions. When an institution provides little training it may be worthwhile taking this deficit up in an appropriate committee, such as student affairs. An alternative is to make a direct approach to a senior member of the academic or administrative staff with a brief to look after student welfare. If a blank is drawn through all these avenues and the tutor wishes to have some specific training it may be worth while approaching student counselling on an individual basis for assistance. If they are not able to offer direct training they may be able to recommend a counselling course run outside the university which will help the tutor develop their interpersonal skills.

Introductory training

An introductory training course for personal tutors is likely to be brief and may take the form of a one- or two-day workshop. It should be held early in the academic year, ideally before students arrive, in order that tutors can begin their preparations. Most courses consist of a mixture of large group seminars and smaller practice workshops.

An introduction to personal tutoring within a specific university will ideally provide first, the opportunity to meet key personnel involved in student welfare, secondly, an outline of the political structure which encompasses student welfare within that institution, and thirdly, basic training in interpersonal communication skills.

The importance of meeting other tutors and welfare personnel has been highlighted previously. An introductory course provides an opportunity for this to occur and for key members of staff to give an outline of their work. If information is not available elsewhere this is the place to find out how students contact agencies such as housing, welfare and student counselling. They may also provide information about the scope of help available, approximate waiting times for appointments, and the mechanism for liaison with tutors. As well as being informed about formal sources of help for students it is useful to know of voluntary helping agencies, including phone lines, both within the university and in the locality.

Interpersonal communication skills
Interpersonal communication skills are not, as is often assumed, inborn. Certainly people vary in the level of sophistication of their communication skills and to a large extent this will be determined by a combination of personality traits and life experiences. To make a broad generalization sociable, outgoing individuals tend to have more interpersonal experience than those who are shy and withdrawn. They are consequently likely to be more confident when speaking to others and to have more highly developed interpersonal skills.

For effective communication to take place three skills are essential. The first is the capacity to speak, to explain, to put over a point of view, an argument or an idea. The second is to be able to listen, to hear, take in and understand what is being said. The third ingredient in a fruitful dialogue is the ability to think, to synthesize information, to change or modify a point of view, and then check out this new thought in further dialogue.

Communication skills training focuses on these three aspects, which incidentally are of great value for the tutors in the academic side of their work as well as in a personal tutoring capacity. Lecturing mainly consists of speaking. Seminars are focused on dialogue. Learning, reading and researching require that an exchange of information, thinking and questioning take place. Therefore the development of communication skills is of potentially great benefit to the academic tutor.

As with all skills development work the central principle underlying communication training is that practice leads to improvement. Learning is facilitated by feedback, which can be incorporated into further practice.

A wide range of techniques are used in training forums. There may be a tutor modelling an 'ideal' personal tutorial, plus an example of a 'disastrous' interview, highlighting common errors or difficulties. Participants may have the opportunity to make a videotape recording of a tutorial and to view this with a small group of peers plus an experienced tutor. This is helpful, as both verbal and non-verbal interchanges can be analysed and tutors can be encouraged to experiment. Through practice they learn which phrases and interventions assist the flow of an interview, and conversely which inhibit dialogue.

Videotape feedback may seem threatening to tutors, who are often nervous about exposure in front of their colleagues. An experienced trainer will help to reduce the anxiety by facilitating constructive feedback and ensuring that everyone in the group takes a turn. Participants are encouraged to follow up any negative comments with a positive suggestion for improvement. The trainer is also able to contribute experiences and ideas about the student problems being presented and so aid thought and discussion in the group. In order to preserve confidentiality interviews which are taped do not usually involve real students with problems. Instead volunteers, who may be actors or workshop participants, role-play students with problems which are based on common experiences.

Example: A student entered the room, sat down and looked at the floor in silence. The tutor said 'Hello', paused for a few seconds and then continued with 'Rotten weather today isn't it?' The student remained immobile and silent. The tutor became restless and fidgety and increasingly uncomfortable until he blurted out 'Well, are you making friends at university?'

After watching a videotape recording of this exchange the tutor was asked to comment on his own interview. He was highly critical of himself and expressed surprise at how abrupt his manner was and of how anxious and ill at ease he seemed. His peers then made some useful suggestions. First, he could have introduced himself to the student in order to help her feel more comfortable. Then instead of making small talk he could have asked a general, open-ended question such as 'How are things with you?' If the student continued to be silent a useful next stage would be to empathize with her and say, 'You seem to be finding it difficult to start talking, I wonder if that's because there is something bothering you.'

This feedback session helped the tutor recognize how he was bringing his own agenda into the room instead of allowing the student to express her concerns. He became less self-critical in response to a recognition by his peers that he was highly motivated to help the student and was trying to put her at ease, however his efforts were not reaching her. He was subsequently able to put the feedback to good use, as shown by a second practice session.

Breaking this down into the three basic skills of speaking, listening, and thinking, the trainer was able to help the tutor recognize that he had started the meeting by 'listening' to what was being conveyed and that his perceptions of this were accurate. In her lack of eye contact and the discomforting silence the student was communicating her distress and difficulty. As the silence continued the anxiety in the room had risen and the tutor's attempt to alleviate this by commenting on the weather had not helped. More than likely it had resulted in the student experiencing that her distress had not been registered, therefore making it even harder for her to begin. The interview became increasingly desperate and the tutor, by now panicking, leapt in with a direct question. Reflecting on it afterwards he was able to see how he had picked up the student's anxiety but was unable to think clearly about how best to help her as he was overwhelmed at the time. By suggesting alternative ways of opening up interviews and by helping him to understand how his thinking had been blocked the trainer was able to facilitate the tutor's interpersonal skills.

This vignette taken from a training session is presented in order that the benefits of such an experience can be appreciated. As with all interpersonal skills reading about them can help but there is no substitute for live exposure, which provides a potent learning medium. We have outlined some basic counselling skills in an earlier chapter where we highlighted the importance of developing rapport, of giving people space by providing time and using open ended questions, of listening, of empathizing, and of communicating clearly to the student.

Training with videotape feedback can be used to improve a wide range of communication skills. It can also be a valuable learning experience to record a practice lecture and review your performance with the help of a trainer and peers. It is useful to know whether your voice can be heard at the back of the lecture theatre, how clear your visual aids are and whether the information you intended to convey was received by your audience. Some universities offer training in teaching skills which incorporate these techniques, usually to good effect.

Further training

Training received on an introductory course may be followed up by subsequent training opportunities. For the majority of tutors further training usually consists of an ongoing forum, for example a group for personal tutors described earlier. This is sometimes enhanced by additional sessional work on interpersonal skills, reinforcing and further refining gains made on an introductory course. These skills are always open to improvement, even in tutors with a wealth of experience.

Additional workshops may focus on areas including working with overseas students, study skills, adolescence, research supervision, the first year experience, and counselling students who fail.

Looking after yourself

One of the major responsibilities of personal tutors is the need to look after themselves. We cannot overstate the importance of this task, which is frequently neglected by individuals. This tendency is enhanced in tutors who have a particularly high sense of responsibility and commitment to their students. Unless tutors are able to look after their own interests they are unlikely to be able to help others. It is therefore essential that tutors ensure that they are able to function effectively.

This attitude is open to accusations of selfishness, however we do not intend to convey the message that tutors' interests should always come first. Instead we propose that they prepare themselves as best they can for their work as tutors, and when involving themselves with students remember that a balance has to be kept between the many demanding aspects of academic posts. In this tutoring has to take its place along with teaching, research, and administration.

One important aspect of tutoring is that limits should be drawn. Tutors are there to help students with problems but it is important to remember that they cannot solve these on behalf of the students, the task of the tutor is to assist the student in finding their own solution. Some students and tutors have difficulty accepting this.

Example: Josephine was struggling with her academic work and falling behind. She had difficulty writing essays and sought help from her tutor. The tutor gave her a number of references which were relevant to the task assigned and three personal tutorial sessions in which he helped Josephine to construct an essay plan. Josephine gained a high grade for the essay and went to see the tutor about the next assignment. She expected to be given considerable help, as had happened previously. The tutor found himself irritated with her for demanding more of his time, but he wanted to help her and again, albeit reluctantly, he assisted her in drafting an essay plan. For the next assignment Josephine again requested help. This time the tutor decided to discuss the request with a colleague.

In discussion the tutor realized that although his intentions were good, in that he wanted to help Josephine learn about the subject that fascinated him, he had not assisted her in developing her study skills. In the tutorials he had done a lot of the required work on Josephine's behalf. He had looked out references and helped her construct an essay plan which she had followed closely. However she had not managed to generalize from their consultations because the work had been done for her.

The tutor arranged a further meeting with Josephine. This time he focused on identifying her difficulties. She had not mastered the library system and therefore was unable to locate relevant articles. She did not understand the process of writing an essay. The tutor's previous interventions had resulted in her feeling helpless and incompetent and now she felt she needed his help even more than ever. He suggested she attend a seminar on the use of the library and referred her to a study skills workshop. For the next assignment he asked her to draft out her own essay plan, then arranged a further tutorial to go through it together and refine it before she wrote the essay. He was now trying to help Josephine by encouraging her to develop study skills rather than by effectively doing the assignment on her behalf.

In this example the tutor wished to help his student but in doing too much for her and by not identifying the core difficulties he compounded the problem. He also placed increased stress on himself by inadvertently encouraging Josephine's dependence on him. Rather than taking care of his own needs by using other resources within the institution he tried to look after his student by giving her a short-term solution to her problems. The problems did not go away, neither did Josephine, and the tutor found the demands on his time escalated.

The essential aspects of tutors looking after their own needs are prioritizing, time management, introductory training, and ongoing review of the work. These have been elaborated in earlier sections of this volume. As outlined here, a realistic assessment of the student's needs can reduce wasted time and ensure they are offered the most appropriate form of help.

An important part of the work of the tutor is to know the resources available in the institution and to ensure students gain access to them. It is not the task of the tutor to meet a student's needs by providing solutions. This is counter-productive in the long term and devalues the student's capacity to solve their own problems. Also, as in the example of Josephine, it can create additional time and emotional pressure for the tutor.

Another mode of working with students is in a group forum, as described in Chapter 3. This has many advantages, especially if specific tasks are tackled when a tutorial can be used to give information to the group. A number of issues central to the task of a tutor can be explored in this setting. These might include an introductory talk, when the tutor outlines arrangements for tutorials and gives information about their function. Other sessions on the use of the library, essay writing, and study skills may follow. Clearly if these subjects are covered by other personnel there is no reason for the tutor to address them with their tutees, but when this is not the case, group tutorial sessions can prove to be a considerable economy of time.

Summary

In this volume we have covered a wide range of aspects relevant to personal tutoring in higher education. We feel that it has in the past been a much neglected task, yet one which is vital to perform well. Using examples from practice we have illustrated the extensive and varied roles encompassed in that of the personal tutor. In doing so we hope to highlight the need for time, training, and reflective thought which are essential for the optimal performance of this task.

Universities pride themselves on the quality of the educational experience they offer to students. These students can be vulnerable, as we have attempted to illustrate. Most of them survive and grow in the atmosphere of learning and it is a pleasure to work with them, to see and share in some of this development. A number do not readily thrive and require help. It is our experience that a little help goes a long way when this occurs. One of the joys of working with this group is that they are in a state of rapid transition and can readily take on board new ideas and put them to good use. The tutor has a valuable role in facilitating this process.

We hope that in drawing together many strands of experience, both of our own and that of other tutors, we have presented information which will be of use to personal tutors. Although we have described many problems within this role we also intended to provide an accurate portrayal of the demands of this work, together with its many rewards. In highlighting the various aspects we have attempted to increase the knowledge base of personal tutors with a view to helping them become more effective in encouraging students' development while simultaneously enhancing their own experience and job satisfaction.

Appendix: Resource Directory

Potential sources of help for students and staff in the community

Local branches of most of the organizations listed here exist in most towns and cities throughout Britain. Information can be gained from central organizations or the telephone directory. There will also be some additional voluntary agencies meeting specific needs. A full local list should be available from a Citizens Advice Bureau, the main library or from the university student advice/welfare centre.

Alcoholics Anonymous
General Service Office, PO Box 1, Stonebow House, Stonebow, York YO1 2NJ, Helpline Tel: 071 352 3001
Support groups for people who want to stop drinking.

British Pregnancy Advisory Service (BPAS)
Austy Manor, Wootton Wawen, Solihull, West Midlands B95 6BX, Tel: 0564 793225
Advice and help for women faced with unwanted pregnancy. Also contraceptive advice, sterilization and infertility help.

Brook Advisory Centre
153a East Street, London SE17 2SD, Tel: 071 708 1390
Confidential contraceptive advice and supplies and counselling for sexual and emotional problems.

Citizens Advice Bureau
National Association of Citizens Advice Bureaux, Myddellton House, 115–123 Pentonville Road, London N1 9LZ, Tel: 071 833 2181
Provides information and advice on a wide range of topics including state benefits, debt, consumer rights and legal help.

CRUSE – Bereavement Care
Cruse House, 126 Sheen Road, Richmond, Surrey TW9 1UR, Tel: 081 940 4818
Offers a service of counselling, advice and opportunities for social contact to all bereaved people.

DIAL UK (Disablement Information and Advice Lines)
Park Lodge, St Catherine's Hospital, Tickhill Road, Balby, Doncaster, South Yorks
DN4 8QN, Tel: 0302 310123
Provides a free, impartial and confidential service of advice and information on all
aspects of disablement to disabled people, carers and professional service providers.

Drugline
9a Brockley Cross, Brockley, London SE4 2AB, Tel: 081 692 4975
Information, advice and counselling for drug related problems.

Gingerbread
35 Wellington Street, London WC2E 7BN, Tel: 071 240 0953
Provides emotional support, practical help and social activities for lone parents and
their children via local self-help groups.

National Aids Helpline
Tel: 0800 567 123
Up-to-date local information about all organisations and individuals who provide
any kind of service related to HIV or Aids.
   There are many local organizations providing services related to HIV or Aids with
different names such as Aidsline, Body Positive, Terence Higgins Trust.

National Council for Civil Liberties
21 Tabard Street, London SE1 4LA, Tel: 071–403 3888
Defence of civil liberties throughout the United Kingdom.

National Association of Young People's Counselling and Advisory Services
(NAYPCAS)
17/23 Albion Street, Leicester LE1 6GD, Tel: 0533 558763
Provides information about counselling services for young people available locally.

National Friend (FRIEND)
BM Friend, London WC1N 3XX
Provides information, advice, support, befriending and counselling to gay, lesbian
and bisexual people and their associates. Affiliated groups throughout Britain.

Pregnancy Advisory Service
13 Charlotte Street, London W1P 1HD, Tel: 071 637 8962
Provides counselling and terminations for people with unwanted pregnancies.

Rape Crisis Centre
No national contact. See local telephone directory.
Provides counselling and support for the victims of rape or sexual assault.

Relate
Herbert Gray College, Little Church Street, Rugby, Warks CV21 3AP, Tel: 0788
73241
Counselling service for people with relationship difficulties.

Scottish Marriage Guidance Council
26 Frederick Street, Edinburgh EH2 2JR, Tel: 031 225 5006
Counselling Service for people with relationship difficulties.

Turning Point
4th Floor, CAP House, 9–12 Long Lane, London EC1A 9AH, Tel: 071 606 3047
A range of services for alcohol and drug related problems, including counselling centres and residential care.

United Kingdom Council for Overseas Student Affairs (UKCOSA)
60 Westbourne Grove, London W2 5SH, Tel: 071 229 9268
Promotes the interests of overseas students in Britain and can provide information and advice.

United Kingdom Immigrants Advisory Service (UKIAS)
County House, 190 Great Dover Street, London SE1 4BY, Tel: 071 357 6917
Counselling and advice for people with immigration problems.

References

Apps, J.W. (1981) *The Adult Learner on Campus.* Follett Publishing, Chicago.

Bion, W.R. (1961) *Experiences in Groups.* Tavistock, London.

Brown, G. and Atkins, M. (1990) *Effective Teaching in Higher Education.* Routledge, London.

Burnham, J.B. (1986) *Family Therapy: First Steps Towards an Integrative Approach.* Tavistock, London.

Erikson, E. (1980) *Identity and the Life Cycle.* W.W. Norton, New York.

Halsey, A.H. (1991) *Decline of Donnish Dominion.* Clarendon, Oxford.

Jaques, E. (1955) 'Social Systems as a Defence Against Persecutory and Depressive Anxiety'. In Klein, M., Heimann, P. and Money-Kyrle, R.E. (eds), *New Directions in Psychoanalysis,* Tavistock, London.

Obholtzer, A. (1989) 'Psychoanalysis and the political process', *Psychoanalytic Psychotherapy,* 4, 55–66.

Rogers, C.R. (1951) *Client Centred Therapy.* Constable, London.

Rudd, E. (1985) *A New Look at Post Graduate Failure.* SRHE and NFER Nelson, Guildford.

Sue, D.W. and Sue, D. (1990) *Counselling the Culturally Different* (2nd edn). John Wiley and Sons, Chichester.

Stephens, A. (1990) *On Jung.* Penguin, Harmondsworth.

Tapper, T. and Salter, B. (1992) *Oxford, Cambridge and the Changing Idea of the University.* SRHE/Open University Press, Buckingham.

The UKCOSA Manual (1989) United Kingdom Council for Overseas Student Affairs, London.

Von Bertalanffy, L. (1968) *General Systems Theory.* Penguin, London.

Von Bertalanffy, L. (1969) 'The Theory of Open Systems in Physics and Biology'. In Emery, F.E. (ed.), *Systems Thinking.* Penguin, Harmondsworth.

Welsh, J. (1979) *The First Year of Postgraduate Research Study.* SRHE, Guildford.

Wolpe, J. (1969) *The Practice of Behaviour Therapy.* Pergamon, New York.

Working with Overseas Students (1990) *A Staff Development Manual.* Published by the Polytechnic of Huddersfield and the British Council.

Index

The Society for Research into Higher Education

The Society for Research into Higher Education exists to stimulate and co-ordinate research into all aspects of higher education. It aims to improve the quality of higher education through the encouragement of debate and publication on issues of policy, on the organization and management of higher education institutions, and on the curriculum and teaching methods.

The Society's income is derived from subscriptions, sales of its books and journals, conference fees and grants. It receives no subsidies, and is wholly independent. Its individual members include teachers, researchers, managers and students. Its corporate members are institutions of higher education, research institutes, professional, industrial and governmental bodies. Members are not only from the UK, but from elsewhere in Europe, from America, Canada and Australasia, and it regards its international work as amongst its most important activities.

Under the imprint *SRHE & Open University Press*, the Society is a specialist publisher of research, having some 55 titles in print. The Editorial Board of the Society's Imprint seeks authoritative research or study in the above fields. It offers competitive royalties, a highly recognizable format in both hardback and paperback and the world-wide reputation of the Open University Press.

The Society also publishes *Studies in Higher Education* (three times a year), which is mainly concerned with academic issues, *Higher Education Quarterly* (formerly *Universities Quarterly*), mainly concerned with policy issues, *Research into Higher Education Abstracts* (three times a year), and *SRHE News* (four times a year).

The Society holds a major annual conference in December, jointly with an institution of higher education. In 1992, the topic was 'Learning to Effect', with Nottingham Polytechnic. In 1993, it was 'Governments and the Higher Education Curriculum: Evolving Partnerships' at the University of Sussex in Brighton, and in 1994, 'The Student Experience' at the University of York. Future conferences include in 1995, 'The Changing University' at Heriot-Watt University in Edinburgh.

The Society's committees, study groups and branches are run by the members. The groups at present include:
Teacher Education Study Group
Continuing Education Group
Staff Development Group
Excellence in Teaching and Learning
Women in Higher Education Group

Benefits to members

Individual

Individual members receive:

* *SRHE News,* the Society's publications list, conference details and other material included in mailings.
* Greatly reduced rates for *Studies in Higher Education* and *Higher Education Quarterly.*
* A 35% discount on all Open University Press & SRHE publications.
* Free copies of the Precedings – commissioned papers on the theme of the Annual Conference.
* Free copies of *Research into Higher Education Abstracts.*
* Reduced rates for conferences.
* Extensive contacts and scope for facilitating initiatives.
* Reduced reciprocal memberships.

Corporate

Corporate members receive:

* All benefits of individual members, plus
* Free copies of *Studies in Higher Education.*
* Unlimited copies of the Society's publications at reduced rates.
* Special rates for its members e.g. to the Annual Conference.

 Membership details: SRHE, 3 Devonshire Street, London W1N 2BA, UK. Tel: 0171 637 2766
Catalogue: SRHE & Open University Press, Celtic Court, 22 Ballmoor, Buckingham MK18 1XW. Tel: (01280) 823388

HELPING AND SUPPORTING STUDENTS
John Earwaker

This book offers a critical review of the various kinds of help and support which institutions of higher education provide for their students. John Earwaker begins by looking at students, their problems, their development, and the way they cope with transitions; these are all to be understood in an interpersonal and social context. He then examines the tutorial relationship, drawing out some of the difficulties and ambiguities in the tutor's role. Finally, he offers an explanation for some of the uncertainty in this area, and sets a new agenda for the future. His recurring theme is that helping students is not some kind of 'extra' which may be tacked on as a supplement to the educational experience but is an integral element in the educational process.

Contents

160pp   0 335 15665 7 (Paperback)   0 335 15666 5 (Hardback)

IMPROVING HIGHER EDUCATION
TOTAL QUALITY CARE

Ronald Barnett

This book provides the first systematic exploration of the topic of quality in higher education. Ronald Barnett examines the meaning of quality and its improvement at the levels of both the institution and the course – contemporary discussion having tended to focus on one or the other, without integrating the two perspectives. He argues against a simple identification of quality assessment with numerical performance indicators *or* with academic audit *or* with the messages of the market. These are the contending definitions of the modern age, but they all contain interests tangential to the main business of higher education.

Dr Barnett offers an alternative approach which begins from a sense of educators attempting to promote and open-ended development in their students. It is this view of higher education which, he argues, should be at the heart of our thinking about quality. Quality cannot be managed, but it can be cared for. Building on the conceptual base he establishes, Dr Barnett offers proposals for action in assessing institutional performance, in reviewing the quality of course programmes, and in improving the curriculum and the character of the student experience.

Contents
Part 1: The idea of quality – The quality of higher education – Aiming higher – The idea of quality – Can quality be managed? – Part 2: Improving the quality of institutions – Institutional purposes and performance indicators – Inside the black box – What's wrong with quality assurance? – Institutions for learning – Part 3: Improving the quality of courses – Practice makes perfect? – Communication, competence and community – We're all reflective practitioners now – Beyond teaching and learning – Conclusions – Appendix – Notes – Bibliography – Index.

256pp   0 335 09984 X (Paperback)   0 335 09985 8 (Hardback)

HELPING STUDENTS TO LEARN
TEACHING, COUNSELLING, RESEARCH

Kjell Raaheim, Janek Wankowski and John Radford

This is a considerably revised and updated edition of a book first published in 1981. This second edition will be as warmly welcomed as the first:

'This vein of rich and reflective experience runs through the whole book, interspersed with a patterning of psychological theory and educational research findings.'

(Studies in Higher Education)

'... it does contain findings which should make all honest academics want to look more closely at their teaching habits and at cherished assumptions about the effectiveness of their contributions. For this reason I should like to see a copy of the book in every university department's library or, better still, in every senior common room.'

(Educational Review)

'Experience, research and vision blend together... The book deserves a wide readership, for it is both scholarly and passionate.'

(British Journal of Guidance and Counselling)

Contents

Teaching and learning: a selective review – From school to university – On the pedagogical skills of university teachers – The need for the development of study skills – The first examinations at university – Success and failure at university – Disenchantment, a syndrome of discontinuity of learning competence – On the vagaries of students' motivations and attitudes to teaching and learning – Assisting the individual student with study difficulties – Reflections and operational prescriptions – Increasing students' power for self-teaching – The teachers and the taught – Bibliography – Name index – Subject index.

192pp   0 335 09319 1 (Paperback)   0 335 09320 5 (Hardback)